CHRISTIAN APOLOGETICS IN A WORLD COMMUNITY

William Dyrness

INTER-VARSITY PRESS
DOWNERS GROVE
ILLINOIS 60515

InterVarsity Press is the book-publishing division of Inter-Varsity Christian Fellowship, a student movement active on campus at hundreds of universities, colleges and schools of nursing. For information about local and regional activities, write IVCF, 233 Langdon St., Madison, WI 53703.

Biblical quotations, unless otherwise indicated, are from the Revised Standard Version of the Bible, copyrighted 1946, 1952, © 1971, 1973.

ISBN 0-87784-399-6

Printed in the United States of America

Library of Congress Cataloging in Publication Data

Dyrness, William A.
    Christian apologetics in a world community.

    Bibliography: p.
    1. Apologetics—History. 2. Apologetics—20th
century. I. Title.
BT1109.D97   1982   239   82-21383
ISBN 0-87784-399-6

---

20   19   18   17   16   15   14   13   12   11   10   9   8   7   6
99   98   97   96   95   94   93   92

*To my Filipino colleagues at the
Institute for Study in Asian Church
and Culture: Manny, Marlon, Melba
and Ruth, whose lives argue for the
truth of Christianity.*

Preface

This book seeks to respond to some of the major challenges that Christianity faces in the modern world. The shape of its argument grew out of my experience of teaching apologetics at Asian Theological Seminary in Manila, though I have modified it for an American audience. One of the burdens of this book is that apologetic argument must grow out of specific contexts; at the same time it is increasingly evident that the major questions facing the church today are global in scope and must be met by a cooperative effort of Christians everywhere. Perhaps this is reason enough for a book written in Asia to be published in North America.

Discussion in this book is more often abstract (or philosophical) than specific and concrete. I have two reasons for choosing this approach. First, many of the challenges facing Christianity are plainly philosophical in character, and there is no way of meeting them adequately except on these terms. Not everyone has to be philosophically trained to defend the faith, but somewhere in our defense we must attempt to grapple with general questions of assumptions and world views. Second, the purpose of this book is more to help the reader develop an apologetic position than to answer specific questions. My general approach will be to develop a strategy of defense against various challenges. I will assess various positions, encouraging the reader to make up his or her own mind. This approach is more difficult than simply listing questions and answers, but it enables the reader in the end to deal with a far wider range of questions than could be touched on in a short book.

This study cannot serve any useful purpose unless the student is thoroughly grounded in Scripture. For it is the Word of God which convinces and convicts unbelievers. The student must first be confronted with the living message which is Jesus Christ and his astounding claims before he or she will know the full meaning of the issues dealt with on these pages.

In order to eliminate footnotes, the author, date (if needed for clarity) and page number of each reference are included in the text. Complete documentation will be found in the bibliography at the back of the book.

While I accrued many debts while preparing this book, I want to mention my indebtedness to the following: my students, whose questions were often better than my answers; my former professor Arthur Holmes of Wheaton College, whose teaching and writing helped shape the direction of this discussion (but whose clarity and insight deserve a better tribute than this book); and Stephen Evans, also at Wheaton, who read the manuscript and offered many helpful suggestions about the arguments I have used. Above all I send the book forth with the prayer that God will raise up a new generation of Christian witnesses in America who will be able to offer a strong and convincing witness that Jesus is Lord.

Quezon City, Philippines
March 1982

PART ONE

Developing an Apologetic Perspective

CHAPTER ONE

Introduction to Apologetics

*T*he word *apologetics* comes from the ancient Greek court, where defendants were given the right to answer or "speak off" the charge brought against them. Plato's *Apology* gives classic expression to such a verbal defense. There the aged Socrates, accused of corrupting the morals of Athens' youth, stands before the people of his city to answer the charge. He pleads with them: "Never mind the manner, which may or may not be good; but think only of the truth of my words, and give heed to that: let the speaker speak truly and the judge decide justly" (p. 60). Peter was perhaps thinking of such a defense when he urged Christians to "always be prepared to make a defense to any one who calls you to account for the hope that is in you, yet do it with gentleness and reverence" (1 Pet 3:15).

The need to defend Christianity against its accusers is as great today as at any other time in its history. On every hand one hears complaints of secularism and tales of the great success of cults and new faiths. Such dangers continue to make apologetics necessary. But we must be careful to keep things in perspective. In one sense today's emphasis on apologetics results more from historical and cultural factors than from religious or philosophical ones. In the curriculum of the medieval seminary (or its equivalent), while there was much vigorous exposition and argumentation of Christianity, apologetics as we know it did not play a major role. The vast majority of the population did not think about defending their faith for the simple reason that they did not think about doubting it. But in the many cultures where the church has lost its controlling influence, Christians have been placed on the defensive and called to answer charges brought against them.

Christians are sometimes sensitive about this role, feeling inadequately prepared to answer sophisticated charges brought against their faith. But in fact defense is not unique to Christianity; all who hold a set of beliefs about life and the world may legitimately be asked to defend themselves. Most problems that Christianity is called upon to face are not unique to the Christian religion, but rather result from our being human. As humans we must think and reason, we must act, and we must commit ourselves to a course of action. Therefore we must be able to defend our commitments. Christians believe that God has revealed himself in human history and has begun a program that people must respond to, but this belief does not exempt Christians from defending themselves like everyone else. They have to understand their faith, become convinced of its truth, fit it together with their experience in the world and then express this reality in responsible action and intelligent communication.

If what we are saying is true, the best apologetic is not a defensive mind-set that sits back and waits for attacks, but a positive expression of what we believe to be true about God, the person and the world. I believe the courage to take the initiative is a gauge of the vitality of our faith. It is a characteristic of evangelicals to be irrepressibly mission oriented, and apologetics should participate in this evangelistic fervor. G. C. Berkouwer has said that apologetics should be seen "not as a defensive movement, but as a courageously ventured witness to the truth in the strength of the Christian faith" (p. 26).

A positive apologetic then will not wait to deal with each challenge as it comes, but will take time to prepare an apologetic viewpoint that can be expected to deal with all challenges. Give a man a fish, goes the proverb, and he will have food for a day; teach him to fish and he will have food for the rest of his life. So in apologetics, it is far more important to build a framework in terms of which objections can be met than to have answers to a large number of questions. The challenges that face Christianity change rapidly and depend on shifting circumstances; thus it is impossible to foresee specific answers we might one day be called upon to give. Our approach in this book will be, in part one, to develop an apologetic perspective from which to examine various kinds of defensive tactics. In part two we will then seek to apply this framework to some important challenges. Our goal will be to develop an overall apologetic strategy.

In this chapter we will briefly discuss the elements of apologetics, which we will more fully develop in chapter three, and then we will deal with some major questions associated with apologetic argument.

Elements of Apologetics
The context. The first element in any defense of Christianity is the context in which the challenger lives. A friend of mine recently recounted an experience he had while teaching apologetics in Africa. He had spent several sessions on arguments for the existence of God when he was approached after class by one of his students. After some hemming and hawing the student finally had the courage to say, "Nobody here really needs to know these arguments for the existence of God. Very few people here doubt that God exists; in fact, they believe in many gods. The question is, which god should we obey?" That professor was getting a

good lesson in the importance of context. Every situation and every culture, indeed every person, has certain implicit needs which the gospel is meant to satisfy. We believe it is a genius of Christianity to be relevant to all human need. It is up to us to be close enough to people to know where these needs exist, to hear the questions that they may not even be able to articulate and to apply the soothing ointment of the gospel just where it is needed.

While teaching in the Philippines I have had experiences similar to that of my friend in Africa. Each time I have taught apologetics I have begun the class by taking a survey of what the class believes to be the most serious challenges to Christianity. What is interesting is the difference not only between these students and those in the West but also between one year and the next. Most recently the major problem was felt to be the irrelevance and impotence of the church. This problem had barely appeared in previous surveys. What had happened to raise this question? Whatever it was, it underlines the need for apologetics to respond to its setting. Christians should be careful not to answer questions no one is asking.

Later we will discuss historical data that indicate that Christianity is true. But even here we must choose evidence that best suits our cultural context. In Western countries abstract biblical themes tend to have an impact: the holiness or righteousness of God, or perhaps his omnipotence. In non-Western countries scriptural evidences of God's power are often more impressive. I have even heard of one case where readers in Africa were most impressed with the Old Testament genealogies. Surely that must be evidence, they felt, for the authenticity of Christianity! Christianity rests on facts, facts that do not change at the whim of the human interpreter. But which facts may count as evidence will depend on the situation in which the reader lives.

The point of view. The second element in any apologetic is a particular point of view, a framework that gives shape to the defense. Here the important element is not factuality, but the consistency that all the facts together are able to express. Here the Christian must take the truths that are found in God's revelation and seek to understand them together. It is the Christian's conviction that the Christian gospel makes sense only in the light of God's character and purposes. Thus an important part of a defense will be understanding the implications of a theistic point of view, that is, a perspective in which God is the creator, sustainer and redeemer of the universe. All must be seen in terms of his will and purposes and the expression of this will in revelation.

We are going to argue that Christianity is not so much an airtight system of irrefutable ideas as it is a perspective, a way of looking at the world. From the Christian perspective, creation expresses God's good purposes; the person uniquely reflects God's own character and thus has infinite value; history tells the story of God's active intervention to restore the order of things corrupted by human selfishness. What the Christian apologist offers is not so much a challenge to listen to our reasons as an invitation to look at the world this way and see it, we believe, as it really is. Respond to things this way, we insist; obey the instructions of the Creator, and everything will begin to make sense for you. As the Bible puts it: "All these things will be added unto you" (Mt 6:33 KJV) and "will work together for good" (Rom 8:28 KJV). If this sounds more like evangelism than apologetics, it simply shows the close relationship between the two.

The starting point. This brings us to that element that we believe must be presupposed in apologetic argument: the starting point. At the risk of oversimplifying a very complex issue, we may introduce this element by asking: Does apologetics seek primarily faith (a commitment and response to God) or reason (an understanding of the faith)? Of course it is impossible to separate these two, for any genuine response involves some understanding, and today we are learning that knowledge must involve nonrational factors. But basically there have been two approaches to apologetics: one emphasizes that we must *understand in order to believe;* the other insists we must *believe in order to understand.* Perhaps it would not be out of place for us to review these approaches at this point.

Members of the first group, those who seek to understand in order to believe, date back to the earliest days of Christian history. Justin the Martyr was one of the first representatives. Justin believed that everything good and true is due to the universal presence of God's truth—what he called the *logos*—and testifies to the truth of Christianity. In the Middle Ages Thomas Aquinas argued that it is possible to know something true about God apart from revelation; in the eighteenth century Joseph Butler believed the principles of morality were intuitively evident to any thinking person. The most important American exponents of this point of view belonged to what is called the Princeton school of theologians. William Brenton Greene and B. B. Warfield may be taken as representatives of this school. Both taught that the role of apologetics as a theological discipline is to establish the presuppositions of systematic theology: the existence of God, the religious nature of people and the truth of historical revelation in Scripture. Greene taught that the idea of the Bible as the Word of God can be established in terms which reason itself must recognize as valid. Reason as a cognitive faculty which compares and judges can be, within its own sphere, a source and ground for religious truth.

Of course neither Greene nor Warfield is saying that reason is infallible, but that before revelation comes, it is the only way we have of investigating truth. Their point is that, if we are not able to lay the foundation of the Christian faith on reasonable grounds, if we cannot show the possibility of miracles or prove the existence of a wise and providential governor, then we may have an unfounded faith. These problems must be capable of resolution on the field of open debate. This is not to say reason can discover the truths of revelation, but it must be able to recognize them. A person may be too sick to find the remedy he needs for his illness, but he may not be unable to recognize and make known what he needs. Faith without evidence is irrational, for faith involves assent, and assent is conviction produced by evidence. Apologetics then must establish the basic truths presupposed in the working out of systematic theology.

Warfield believed that the Holy Spirit is necessary to produce saving faith, but that reason can produce the grounds for such faith. As he put it, "Rational argumentation does, entirely apart from that specific operation of the Holy Ghost which produces saving faith, ground a genuine exercise of faith" (p. 115). The assent then which the Holy Spirit produces is not different in kind but in degree from that which is possible apart from the Spirit. What the Spirit does is to turn assent into a faith which results in the glad and loving trust of a regenerated person. Christianity, Warfield believed, "has been placed in the world to reason its way to the dominion of the world. And it is by reasoning its way that it has come to Kingship" (p. 120).

Much can be said for this point of view. People are rational beings and must be given reasons for believing something is true. Still one may wonder, even if reasoning of some sort must come first, whether the important element in apologetics is not the commitment rather than the reasons, whether in fact any reasoning can take place outside of some faith commitment. The second group, those who believe in order to understand, addresses these questions.

The second approach also has representatives in the early periods of Christian history. Augustine and Anselm both used the phrase *Believe in order to understand.* They could have entitled their apologetic program *Faith Seeking Understanding.* The heirs of this tradition include John Calvin, Blaise Pascal and, in the last century, Abraham Kuyper. According to Kuyper, apologetics should only defend what is given in systematics. Faith is the primary category. This faith Kuyper calls "an action by which our consciousness is forced to surrender itself, and to hold something for true . . . and to obey something" (p. 127). One must in fact be certain before giving or accepting a demonstration. Faith is the presupposition of all demonstration. Since sin has affected our whole nature, nothing can ultimately prove, for example, that Scripture is the means of our salvation:

Even though it were frankly granted that something is lacking in our reason, that our reason by itself is insufficient—yes, that it calls for a complement—the conclusion can never be logically drawn from this that Sacra Scripture . . . either is or offers this complement. . . . The dispute can advance no further than the acknowledgement of antinomies in our consciousness and the insufficiency of our reason to satisfy entirely our thirst after knowledge. . . . All the trouble, therefore, that men have given themselves to make advance, by logical argument, from the acknowledgement of the insufficiency of our reason as a starting-point, has been a vain expenditure of strength. (pp. 384-85)

Kuyper of course does not deny that reason will play a role in conviction, but this will always be a secondary role. "The witness of the Holy Spirit is and ever will be the only power which can carry into our consciousness the certainty concerning the special principium [Scripture]" (p. 388).

Warfield objects that Kuyper's procedure first explicates the system and only then asks if it is fact or fiction. This Warfield believes leads inevitably to mysticism, a charge often levelled against those who do not allow reason to play a primary (or we may say autonomous) role. Members of this second school respond that when the role of reason is exaggerated, the danger of rationalism is present.

The differences between these points of view may be partly due to different definitions of apologetics. The first approach holds that a rational demonstration of the content of belief is possible apart from the working of the Holy Spirit; apologetics then is strictly a work of reason. The second approach, on the other hand, ties apologetics closely to evangelism as part of the process of persuading people to accept Christ as Lord. While we will assume the second approach throughout this study, we will also attempt to show that giving faith—the commitment of the whole person to the self-revelation of God—the primary place does not in the least depreciate reason and evidence, but rather shows them their proper and essential place. The thesis of this book is that God requires a total response involving mind, will and imagination actively participating in his ongoing program. We are to do as well as to acknowledge his will; we are to show as well as to trust his character; and we are to obey as well as to accept his Word. The various kinds of argumentation this implies will be more fully developed in chapter three. Meanwhile we turn our attention to questions we may have as we approach the study of apologetics.

Questions about Apologetics

What does a Christian defend? When they examine the history of the church, Christians may wonder what they are called upon to defend. After all many things done in the name of Christ are not defensible by any standard. Jude 3 gives an answer to this question: We are to "contend for the faith which was once for all delivered to the saints." It is the truth contained in Scripture, "the faith" that we are to express and defend. Occasionally events in the history of the church can be used to illustrate a truth of Scripture. We are not called upon, however, to defend everything that goes under the name *Christian*. It is the truth of revelation, what the Bible refers to as that quick and powerful Word of God (Heb 4:12), which we must seek to present in all its clarity. For it is this which produces conviction and new life.

But is it really necessary to defend Christianity? If the gospel is the power of God unto salvation, who are we to seek to defend it? After all a lion does not need to be defended; it need only be released. There is certainly some evidence for the view that apologetics is not really necessary. Martin Luther, responding to those who asked what he had done to cause all that trouble in Germany, once said:

> I simply taught, preached, and wrote God's Word; otherwise I did nothing. And while I slept . . . the Word so greatly weakened the papacy that no prince or emperor ever inflicted such losses upon it. I did nothing; the Word did everything. (4:241)

One modern apologist, Cornelius van Til, insists that preaching is the best apologetic. But while we have seen that reason cannot play a primary role in coming to faith, it does play an important role. If it is not a sufficient cause for faith, it is a necessary condition for it. While it may be true that no one was ever argued into the kingdom of God, it is also true that no one became a Christian without some reason. As we will see momentarily, the Holy Spirit plays a crucial role, but he works in and through reason. The Holy Spirit uses truth to quicken and restore.

Does sin make reason unreliable? Though it is true that sin affects all that a person does, including reasoning, it is not true that he or she cannot understand truth when it is presented. The image of God was not entirely lost with the Fall; theologians have included this ability to understand truth among the benefits of common grace. While the illumination of the Holy Spirit is necessary to faith, it is the truth of Christianity that is illumined, and it is this truth we must contend for.

Who needs apologetics? Christians or non-Christians or both? Of course we think first of non-Christians, for they are more likely to bring objections against the faith. How then is apologetics related to preaching? It is clear that ordinarily people come to Christ by preaching. Paul says: "For since . . . the world did not know God through wisdom, it pleased God through the folly of what we preach to save those who believe" (1 Cor 1:21). This folly —what the New Testament calls the scandal of the gospel—is a stumbling block for many people; they cannot accept it even when it is clearly presented and understood, and no apologetic argument can remove this obstacle. But for many people it is not the folly of the gospel that is offensive, but some other scandal connected with Christianity. They may be attracted to Communism and wonder if Christianity has any comparable program for human development. They may be troubled by the problem of evil: how can a good God let innocent people suffer? They may have studied philosophy and wonder how Christianity can be understood in philosophical categories. All these challenges can and must be met. All the outer defenses against the gospel must be taken down so that the truth may penetrate into the heart of the city. Apologetics has a role to play then in clearing the ground for belief, removing obstacles that may stand in the way and preparing the way for evangelism. To do this we must always face honest questions and strive to give thoughtful responses.

But apologetics has a role to play in the life of the believer as well. A modern theologian, Paul Tillich, has argued that there is an element of doubt in the faith of every person. Perhaps it is a result of being human that every now and then we have serious questions about our faith that we must face. Part of growth in the Christian life involves facing squarely these questions as they come and doing our best to answer them. Apologetics, Bouillard says, is "an essential character and one of the permanent conditions of faith" (p. 12).

Looked at in this light, apologetic activity is a sign of the vigor of Christian faith. It has always been a source of encouragement to me as a teacher of apologetics that we place such importance on meeting objections. Apologetics is often a required course in Bible school and seminary curricula. Many of these courses aim simply to find and meet any and all challenges to Christianity. Is there a problem that we feel? Has someone brought a charge against the faith? Let us examine each one and consider how best we might respond. A vigorous Christianity cannot survive unless such challenges are honestly faced.

What are the place of revelation and the role of the Holy Spirit in apologetics? Obviously Scripture is the norm for our defense just as it is for all other areas of our faith and practice. But the Bible does not come to us in a form that answers all our questions. God consistently adapted revelation to meet our human condition, and that means he revealed himself to us in particular historical and cultural forms that we must learn to interpret. Apologetics can give us questions with which to approach Scripture, but we must have the patience to apply ourselves carefully to the language and structure of Scripture in order to hear what is being said to us.

The Scriptures furnish a norm for apologetic discussion in two ways. First, they speak of particular events which when properly interpreted are saving events. They provide unique and sufficient instances of God's saving self-revelation. Beginning with creation and leading to the predicted consummation, these events are constitutive for Christian life and history. We must find our personal bearings in this story. Second, these events and their inspired interpretation provide us with points of reference that shape and mold our thinking. They enable us to understand the centrality of God, the goodness of creation and the sad influence of sin, to name only some basic themes. These themes provide us with a frame of reference in which to think about apologetics. But we cannot construct an adequate frame of reference without outside assistance.

Here is where the work of the Holy Spirit comes in. The Spirit is given us to witness to Christ and the truth of revelation. But he does not minister in a vacuum. He does not whisper answers in our ear while we sit with the Bible open before us. He works in and through the careful exegesis of Scripture, providing a continuing prophetic critique of our life and thought, applying the truth to our hearts and, as John Calvin liked to put it, subduing our hearts to teachableness. Neither does the Holy Spirit make reason and evidence unnecessary; rather he works in and through them to make the light shine and to allow us to submit to the evidence that is there. Let us not spare ourselves as we seek to intelligently defend the faith, but let us not have an exaggerated sense of the importance of argument. We simply must do what we can and wait prayerfully on the Lord to do what he wills.

Questions for Review
1. What is the source of the word *apology?*
2. What verse authorizes our apologetic endeavors?
3. How can apologetics be a positive expression of Christian witness?
4. Describe briefly the three elements of apologetics.
5. Describe the view that faith is primary and reason secondary in apologetic discussion.
6. How does the Holy Spirit work in relation to reason and revelation?
7. How does apologetics function for the Christian?
8. How does it function for the non-Christian?
9. Explain the role of reason and evidence in bringing a person to Christ.

CHAPTER TWO

Historical Sketch of Apologetics

*I*n this chapter we will briefly examine the history of Christian apologetics. We must never think that we alone in Christian history have been called to defend our faith. We are a part of a discussion that has lasted almost two thousand years. We all in fact are products of earlier discussions. Let us then consider some examples from Christian history that illustrate various types of argument, in order to learn from them and to build on their foundation.

The New Testament
From the very beginning Christians have been called upon to defend their faith that Jesus is the Messiah, the Son of God. Recent study shows that each Gospel is seeking to defend a particu-

lar point of view. Matthew was probably written to demonstrate Christ's Old Testament heritage and his authority as a Jewish savior. Mark focuses on the character of Jesus' own defense of his ministry (see Mark 2:10-11 and 28). Luke and Acts were written for an educated Roman, Theophilus, and may have had as part of their purpose to respond to the accusation that Christians were disloyal to Roman authority. John states his purpose clearly in 20:31: "These are written that you may believe that Jesus is the Christ." Perhaps an auxiliary purpose of his was to comfort Christians who were under attack by Jewish propaganda. Throughout the New Testament we see the apostles having to respond to attacks on three different fronts, from Judaism, Greek thought and the Roman Empire (see Bruce).

Confrontation with Judaism. The first challenge was purely religious: to persuade the Jews that Jesus, who suffered an ignominious death, was the Messiah predicted by the Old Testament prophets. From the very first, the apostles proclaimed publicly that by raising Jesus from the dead, God had kept his promises to David (Acts 2:32-36 and 13:34). As Jesus explained to the travelers on the road to Emmaus, his sufferings were part of God's plan of glorifying his servant (Lk 24:26-27). It was therefore necessary for the apostles to meet head on the offense associated with Christ's death on the cross. Paul responded by using the Old Testament idea of a curse resting on one who does not keep the law (compare Deut 21:23 and 27:26 with Gal 3:10, 13). In an argument reminiscent of the rabbinic style, he showed that Christ had to bear the curse of lawbreakers by dying on the cross.

Why then did the Jewish people not welcome the Messiah when he came? The early Christians had two answers. On the one hand they showed that Jesus' rejection was itself prophesied (see Mk 7:6-8 referring to Is 29:13). On the other hand they pointed out that in their day as in Old Testament times there was a believing remnant (Is 11:11, Rom 11:5). In all their preaching and teaching they moved with perfect confidence through the Old Testament. Here they found the rationale for their faith that in Christ God had acted decisively for the salvation of humankind and that as a result, they now lived in the last days.

A word more is in order about the apostles' use of the Old Testament. The first Christians had no doubt that the life and ministry of Christ fulfilled the Old Testament. They felt that if something could not be proved from the Old Testament, it could not be proved at all. No doubt taking their cue from the Lord himself who constantly referred to the Scriptures, the apostles searched the entire Old Testament to support their contention that God had acted for humanity's salvation in Jesus of Nazareth. The book of Hebrews, for example, rests its whole argument on certain key Old Testament texts (see Lindars).

Confrontation with Greek thought and paganism. Beginning in Acts 11 we see a new element in missionary preaching: Christians facing the Greek attitude that the cross as a means of salvation is simple foolishness. Here begins the long and variegated contact between Christianity and Greek philosophy. Salvation to well-educated Greeks involved an intellectual quest for knowledge of the ideal. Their cyclical view of history made it impossible for them to imagine that God could reveal himself in the changing forms of visible reality. Paul meets this objection head on in 1 Corinthians 1:18-25. Whatever human minds may think of it, he says, this particular death was God's way of making his power manifest.

In his sermons at Lystra and Athens, Paul uses a wholly new approach that focuses on natural revelation (see Acts 14:8-18 and 17:22-31). He begins with God, the Creator of the natural order, and with people who seek to know and worship him. Now, Paul says, by the death and resurrection of Christ, God calls all people to repent and turn to him. Interestingly, it is the mention of the resurrection that proves too much for Paul's audience, and they begin to laugh. Resurrection to a Greek was preposterous, for bodily existence, to a Greek, was a hindrance from reaching full spiritual potential. Yet Paul sometimes succeeded in his ministry among Greeks; in 1 Thessalonians 1:9-10 Paul acknowledges "what a welcome we had among you, and how you turned to God from idols, to serve a living and true God."

Confrontation with the Roman Empire. The conflict between Christians and the Roman state began as simply the extension of the conflict between Jews and their secular rulers. Christ gave the basic principles in Mark 12:14-17: each authority had its proper sphere and was to be honored in its place. The early church especially cherished this word of Christ, perhaps because it had so often been accused of disloyalty. Christians could not honor Caesar the way others did. They could not extol the empire and its gods. They worshiped a man who had been executed by Roman authorities on a charge of sedition. Tensions between church and state were thus inevitable, and they threatened the young church at every turn. This may account for the explicit comments in 1 Peter 2:13-17 and in Romans 13:7. Paul's remarks in Romans may have been made to demonstrate his good faith in anticipation of his visit to that city. His appeal to Caesar may have been a part of a program designed to win a favorable hearing for the gospel by Roman authorities.

The Early Church
In the period immediately following the writing of the New Testament, there was little apologetic concern with the surrounding pagan world. The Apostolic Fathers were first intent upon consolidating the scattered but growing Christian communities. Only during the next generations did the so-called Apologists begin to respond to challenges that came their way. They had to face attacks from philosophers, from emperors and other rulers, and of course from the Jews.

The most famous Apologist is Justin the Martyr (ca 100-ca 165), who was born in Palestine and ended his life as a Christian teacher in Rome. We have two apologies from his hand which seek to answer the popular anti-Christian slander. He says: "It is for us, therefore, to offer to all the opportunity of inspecting our life and teachings, lest we ourselves should bear the blame for what those who do not really know about us do in their ignorance" (*First Apology* 3). He tried to show that the wise philosophers were able to come to understand truth because of the Word (*logos*) speaking to them. But all the wonderful things that Plato was able to discern are presented more clearly in God's revelation of himself. As a result among Christians "you can hear and learn these things from those who do not even know the letters of the alphabet—uneducated and barbarous in speech, but wise and faithful in mind—even from cripples and the blind. So you can see that these things are not the product of human wisdom, but are spoken by the power of God" (*First Apology* 60).

It is the quality of the Christians' life that is their strongest defense, Justin insists, even if Christians are unimportant in the eyes of the world. At the same time that Justin was writing, Celsus, a Greek writer, launched what was perhaps the first systematic attack against Christianity. He may have been thinking of Justin when he retorted that Christians depend on classical wisdom, but they always distort what they use. They celebrate feasts as if God were enriched by their gifts; they worship a god who became a man (did he leave heaven empty?). Worst of all from his point of view was the type of people attracted to Christianity.

> Let us hear what kind of persons those Christians invite. Everyone, they say, who is a sinner, who is devoid of understanding, who is a child and to speak generally, whoever is unfortunate—him will the kingdom of God receive. (Quoted in *Contra Celsus* 3.59)

We would never have heard of this "famous" Greek writer if, about seventy years later, a Christian scholar by the name of Origen had not written an answer to his charges. One of Origen's converts had come across Celsus's work and persuaded Origen to reply. Origen reluctantly agreed, and the result is the famous apologetic tract *Contra Celsus*. Origen explained that God is not enriched by Christian feasts but is honored as the Lord of all human days. God descended to earth because of his great love and his desire to meet human need where it exists. As to the ragtag collection of people who have come to drink the living water, Origen had this to say:

> Christ is the Savior of all men whether they be intellectual or simple; those that are instructed and wise can come here and

be satisfied; those that are foolish or sick or sinful can approach in order to be cured. (Ibid.)
How surprised Celsus would have been had he lived to read such a distinguished reply to his spiteful attack.

Another important early defense of Christianity is the *Apology* of Tertullian written about A.D. 197. Tertullian continues the emphasis that Christians prove by their lives the truth of their faith. Noting that Christians have been accused of immorality, infanticide and even atheism (because they do not worship the Roman gods), he asks why Christians are condemned without investigation of their deeds. Why, he wonders, are all kinds of deities lawful except the one good God of the Christians? The Egyptians are even allowed to deify birds and kill anyone who touches them. In the end it is the Christians' way of life, Tertullian maintains, that shows the validity of their beliefs: goodness is their identifying characteristic. They hold everything in common (except their wives, he notes wryly). Above all Christians choose to believe, even at the risk of martyrdom. Tertullian concludes: "We become more numerous everytime we are hewn down by you: the blood of Christians is seed" (*Apology* 50).

It was Tertullian who asked the famous question, "What has Athens to do with Jerusalem?" Perhaps it would be fitting to say a word about his deprecation of philosophy. This question occurs in the context of Tertullian's argument (in the *Prescription against Heretics*) that truth is to be found in the churches which teach Scripture. In Scripture, says Tertullian, we find an orderly system of truth laid down by Christ. We have formulated this truth into the rule of faith (an early creed or confession). Since we have the truth we need no longer seek after it. Thus we have no need for philosophy, which, for Tertullian, is a seeking after truth; philosophy, in fact, in the churches merely equips heretics. So for Tertullian Christianity and philosophy are as distinct as faith and speculation.

Not everyone in the early church had such a negative view of philosophy. Both Justin and Origen used philosophical elements in their apologetic, and Augustine, to whom we now turn, gave

Christianity a philosophical expression that molded theology for eight hundred years. Augustine (ca 354-430), a native of North Africa, eventually became the bishop of Hippo. After more than a decade of dissolute living and wandering in Neo-Platonic philosophy, Augustine had been converted as a result of Ambrose's preaching in Milan. Of his several contributions to apologetics, two stand out for their continuing influence on Christians. The first is contained in his *Confessions* (written shortly before 400), the first great spiritual autobiography and one of the classics of Christian literature. Here he lays out a wholly new program for the elucidation of faith. Following the philosopher Plato rather than emphasizing objective factors, Augustine begins with ideas in the mind. In his view God is found within:

> Thus doth the soul commit fornication, when she turns from thee, seeking without thee, what she findeth not pure and untainted, till she returns to Thee. . . . Let them then be turned, and seek thee; because not as they have forsaken their creator, hast thou forsaken thy creation. Let them be turned and seek thee; and behold, thou art there in their heart, in the heart of those who confess to thee, and cast themselves upon thee, and weep in thy bosom, after all their rugged ways. (pp. 27, 65)

The knowledge of God is thus not a result of inference but is an immediate experience of the soul. Augustine certainly did not despise reason; in fact he insisted that a criterion for truthfulness resides within the mind. But truths that we can reflect on are important because they imply an unchanging Truth, God himself, underlying all that we know of truth and beauty. "For these lower things have their delights, but not like my God, who made all things; for in him doth the righteous delight, and he is the joy of the upright in heart" (p. 25).

While everyone may enjoy and understand something of the delights of these lower things, in Augustine's view only the one who knows God can appreciate them properly. Hence his famous dictum: "If you are not able to know, believe that you may know. Faith precedes; the intellect follows" (*Sermons* 98, 1). To learn anything, Augustine believed, one must be open to truth, and to be open to the truth as it exists in God's creation is to be open to God. Only through God's presence and his illumination are we able to know truth at all. For this we need to have faith, to repose in the presence of God and to open our eyes to see what he would reveal. Faith, then, far from restricting the intellect, rather provides the condition in which reason can freely operate. Philosophy and reason can then be put into the service of faith, establishing all that faith accepts. Augustine put it this way:

> Since the mind, which was meant to be reasonable and intelli-
> gent, has, by dark and inveterate vices, become too weak to
> adhere joyously to his unchangeable light (or even to bear it)
> until, by gradual renewal and healing, it is made fit for such
> happiness, its first need was to be instructed by faith and puri-
> fied. (1958, II. 2)

Augustine's second major contribution in apologetics is found in his great defense of a Christian view of history, the *City of God,* written about A.D. 413-26. In 410 the city of Rome fell to Alaric the Goth and the great empire seemed doomed. Some people were quick to blame the calamity on Christianity, which had largely superseded the ancient Roman religion. Augustine accepted the challenge and wrote this classic response. In books 1-10 he argued that the worship of false gods has never contributed to the prosperity of human affairs. Why should the gods that failed to save Troy help Rome in its hour of need? When in fact did pagan gods ever intervene to help their people? By contrast, the Christian God is everywhere present and active in power; no place can exclude him.

Beginning in book 11, Augustine turns from the defensive to develop a positive case for Christianity. All things are under the universal providence of God who sent his Son to provide eternal life. To understand history one must recognize the continuing struggle between two cities, one ruled by pride and self-love and one ruled by God's love. "The two cities spring from two different kinds of love, the earthly from love of self leading to contempt of God, and the heavenly from love of God leading to contempt of self" (14.28). So Augustine projects his insight about individual spiritual struggle onto the plane of history and sees there a reflection of human selfishness and injustice. This is a major advance. Not every Christian would be satisfied with Augustine's psychological view of history, but his basic insight is beyond doubt: The events of history may or may not provide a justification for Christianity, but it can be shown that Christianity provides an adequate basis for an understanding of history.

The Middle Ages
In the Middle Ages in Europe, there was need not so much to defend the faith as to build up those who already believed. Two of the major thinkers, Anselm and Thomas Aquinas, both concerned to commend the faith to believers, nevertheless represent quite different approaches to apologetics.

Anselm of Canterbury (ca 1033-1109) continued Augustine's emphasis on believing reason. In the *Proslogion* (1078-79), where he develops his famous ontological argument for the existence of God, he admits: "For this too I believe, that 'unless I believe, I shall not understand' " (*Pros.* 1). He goes on to argue that for one who believes in God, his existence is seen as necessary; if we can imagine a perfect being, this being must exist or he would be imperfect. Anselm develops the idea of God as Christians understand him. He counsels:

Now then little man, for a short while fly from your business; hide yourself for a moment from your turbulent thoughts. Break off now your troublesome cares, and think less of your laborious occupations. Make a little time for God, and rest for a little while in him. Enter into the chamber of your mind, shut out everything but God and whatever helps you to seek him, and, when you have shut the door, seek him. Speak now O my whole heart, speak now to God: I seek thy face; thy face Lord, do I desire. (*Pros.* 1)

Reason, like faith, is a gift of God. If faith convinces a person of the truth of God's self-sufficiency, surely reason will be able to demonstrate that truth. Whether Anselm actually believed that his ontological proof was capable of convincing unbelievers has been much debated by theologians. At least we can agree with the assessment of E. L. Mascall: "If God is what faith assures us he is, he is of such a nature that reason should be able to prove his existence" (p. 207). Anselm here demonstrates what Augustine had desired, that reason should be able to show by logic what faith has accepted as true.

Another example of this kind of reasoning is found in Anselm's great work *Why God Became Man* (1098), where he seeks to show why it is reasonable for God to become man in order to bring salvation. God's intention, he argues, was to perfect human nature. He did this by sending a perfect man, Jesus, whose pure death is able to outweigh all possible sins. Here Anselm gives classic expression to our understanding of Christ's death: "God did require from man that he should conquer the devil, and that he who had offended God by sin should make satisfaction by justice" (*Why God Became Man*, p. 19). This he accomplished by the perfect sacrifice of Christ. It is not hard to see why Anselm stands as one of the most important Christian thinkers in the history of the church, for he made it his goal always to give a reason and explanation of the hope that God had given him. He sought to show the inner structure and rationality of the Christian truth that faith accepts.

The second major medieval thinker has been even more influential than Anselm on the history of apologetics. Thomas Aquinas (ca 1225-74) has become the major philosophical influence for many Christians, especially in the Catholic Church. His two major works are the *Summa Theologica* (1265-73) and the *Summa contra Gentiles* (1261-64). The latter was written as a textbook for missionaries and contains his important defense of natural theology (that is, theology that can be known apart from Scripture). It was directed chiefly against the views of Arabian Moslems. Aquinas introduces his position:

> In those things which we assert of God, the way of truth is twofold. For there are things which we assert of God which surpass every faculty of human reason—that he is triune, for example. But there are others which are within the scope of nat-

ural reason, such as that he exists, that he is one, and others of this kind; these have been proved by philosophers, following the light of reason. (SCG, 1.3)
This statement of the two ways to truth carries important implications. For both Augustine and Anselm, philosophy clearly played an auxiliary role to theology. Now with Aquinas philosophy is made to stand on its own feet, capable of discovering truth by the exercise of reason alone, independent of special revelation. (Some people believe that the beginning of modern philosophy with its emphasis on the autonomy of human reason is to be found in Aquinas.)

A word needs to be said about Aquinas's philosophical framework. The philosophy of Aristotle had recently been discovered, and Aquinas was influenced by this thinker in several significant ways. Most important, he accepted Aristotle's basic empirical orientation: he believed that knowledge is primarily a result of experience and sensation. Plato, we have seen, had emphasized knowledge as a matter of ideas; this rationalism was influential on Augustine and also on Anselm. For Aristotle, on the other hand, knowledge is based on sensory experience. Aquinas accepted this premise. From our knowledge of the external world, he maintained, we can *infer* the existence of God.

Aquinas works out this position in his great *Summa Theologica*. It was his view that God's nature is self-evident in itself, but since we cannot know this nature immediately, it is not self-evident to us. We are limited to our experience of the material world whose character must always condition our knowledge. So whereas Augustine began with ideas in his mind, Aquinas began with the material world. Since God is the cause of everything that exists, we are able to find out about him by his effects, the created order we live in.

Here Aquinas developed his famous five ways to knowledge about God. We understand motion; there must be a first mover. We understand efficient cause; there must be a first cause. We see possibility and necessity; since there is something rather than nothing, something must exist necessarily. We know of gradation of goods; there must be some final good that is the cause of these lesser goods. We believe that all things act for an end; there must be a governor controlling these purposes (ST. I, Q 2 Art.3). These arguments have been much debated, and today few Christians would subscribe to them as they stand. But if God has created the world and continues to sustain it, we should be able to learn something about him from the created order. We should find there, as the medieval theologians liked to say, vestiges of God. But Aquinas had something more in mind. He is not only saying that we can know something of God from the world, but that in some important sense God is present in his creation; thus our knowledge of the world can be a vehicle of our knowledge of God. As creatures of time and space we must be able to come to God in and through the material order that is the condition of our human existence. The corollary of this is that God should be able to come to us this way as well, which is just what the teaching of the Incarnation affirms.

Aquinas's teaching here had a great deal of influence in the Middle Ages, especially among the mystics. This passage from Julian of Norwich, a fourteenth-century English mystic, gives us a similar view:

> [God] showed me a little thing, the size of a hazelnut, lying in the palm of my hand. . . . I looked at it with the eyes of my understanding and thought, "What can this be?" My question was answered, . . . "It is everything that is made." I marveled how this could be, for it seemed to me that it might suddenly fall into nothingness, it was so small. An answer for this was given to my understanding: "It lasts and ever shall last, because God loves it. And in this fashion all things have their being by the grace of God." In this little thing I saw three properties. The first is that God made it. The second is that God loves it. The third is that God keeps it. (Chap. 5)

The goal of the Christian life for Aquinas is a pure vision of God unencumbered by material intermediaries. Such a vision is not possible in its fullness until we stand before God, but mystical experiences can anticipate it, and even our experience in creation gives us glimpses of this vision.

To be able to experience God properly through the created order, however, we need what Aquinas called the second way of truth: revelation. Some things about God obviously cannot be known from experience or are so rarely discovered that outside assistance is necessary. For this God gives us special revelation in Scripture. There we find the truths that reason cannot discover—the Trinity, Incarnation and the sacraments—which are necessary for the systematic knowledge of theology. Revealed truth is proven not by argument from the nature of things but from evidence that Scripture is a revelation from God: miracles, prophecy and the like. The goal of this truth is to lead us to salvation, and it must be accepted by faith. Faith is not a blind act of the will; it is an act of the intellect, a thinking with assent.

Significant for our purposes is that all of Aquinas's theology is oriented toward the knowledge of God. Faith is a submission of the mind to God's revelation of himself; even the vision of God in heaven is an intellectual illumination of God's essence. How much Aquinas is indebted to the Greek heritage where the goal of human life is knowledge is clear. But is human failure a lack of knowledge, or is it rather as Augustine had insisted a perverted will?

The Reformation

Here the Reformers broke with their medieval predecessors, for the Reformers began with a sense of moral rather than intellectual need. Thus they were far less concerned about reasoning toward faith than about accepting the grace they believed God was holding out to them. The Reformers did almost no apologetics in the usual sense of the word. Their main concern was to formulate the gospel in a purified form while attacking the abuses in the Catholic Church which had obscured this joyous offer.

Martin Luther (1483-1546), an Augustinian monk, started his religious quest with the question: How do I find a gracious God? Seeing the perfect God and fallen human nature as enemies, he concluded that we are reconciled to God only through God's gracious coming to man in the gospel. We can know God only as he dresses himself in his Word and promises. Because of his belief in the primacy of the gospel, Luther often sounded as if he distrusted reason. In his commentary on Galatians he sounds like Tertullian when he says: "Reason, thou art foolish. . . . So the godly by faith kill such a beast . . . and thereby do offer to God a most acceptable sacrifice and service." In truth Luther did not believe that reason was useless to the Christian, but that the gospel can do without our defense:

> We must take care not so to deface the Gospel (not by its own strength but by our powers) that it is quite lost, to defend it so well that it collapses. Let us not be anxious: the Gospel needs not our help; it is sufficiently strong in itself. God alone commends it, whose it is. . . . Therefore it is a small wretched thing that this puny breath should range itself against the sophists: what would this bat accomplish by its flapping? (Sermon on Faith and Good Works, in Reid, p. 131)

In the context of faith, however, when the dragon of unbelief had been slain, reason could be seen in another perspective. Reason in "a man of faith, regenerate and enlightened by the Holy Spirit through the Word, . . . is a fair and glorious instrument and work of God. . . . The understanding, through faith, receives life from faith; that which was dead is made alive again" (*Table Talk*, Hazlitt, par. 294). In matters which concern faith, reason can be useful when it is enlightened by faith. What Luther opposed was not reason as such but the attempt to use reason in making a ladder to climb up to heaven.

We are in a wholly different atmosphere with John Calvin (1509-64), but his conclusions are surprisingly close to Luther's. Calvin was trained as a lawyer in the Renaissance humanist tradition and never outgrew his love for beauty of expression and for the ancient traditions, though his estimation of these things was changed by his conversion. He never spoke against reason in the way Luther did. Unlike Aquinas, he saw reason not so much as weak as turned in on itself. His account of his conversion helps to explain his position:

God by a sudden conversion subdued and brought my mind to a teachable frame, which was more hardened in such matters than might have been expected from one at my early period of life. Having thus received some taste and knowledge of true godliness, I was immediately inflamed with so intense a desire to make progress therein, that although I did not altogether leave off other studies, I yet pursued them with less ardour. (Preface to *Commentary on the Psalms*)

Calvin's view of reason and argument grew out of his conviction that there is no true knowledge of self apart from the knowledge of God. But in spite of the human inclination to seek God and the daily disclosure of God through creation, it is only through his Word and the working of the Spirit in us that we can have a true knowledge of God. Scripture gives us the means to know God aright, and there are evidences to support its truth if we have eyes to see them: beauty of language, prophecy and miracle, and the preservation of the Bible. But Calvin never believed these evidences could provide the primary confirmation for our faith; this must come from the Holy Spirit illuminating our minds.

If these references imply that during the Reformation advances in the field of apologetics were slight, such a conclusion would be misleading. Principles were established then that were later to have far-reaching effects, not all beneficial. The Reformers insisted that a person is justified by faith alone, that he approaches God alone, and that his status with God, though depending on God alone, reflects his decision of faith. All this was liberating when seen in its biblical context, but when taken out of that context it could prove dangerous.

The Age of Rationalism

When the wars of religion finally ended in Europe in 1648, people were anxious that religion be a means of advancing civilization and not something to fight over. Imperceptibly a new critical attitude was gaining ground as inductive and empirical methods of inquiry were emphasized. Science and travel were opening up a whole new world and humanity felt on the verge of many exciting possibilities. Throughout, a confidence in the ability of reason grew alongside a new tolerance for different points of view. John Locke (1632-1704) may be taken as representative of this period. In Locke's view, human understanding is too limited for one man to impose his beliefs on another; the Christian church therefore should be broad enough to allow for individual opinions. In his famous *Essay Concerning Human Understanding* (1690), he argues that all knowledge must come through sensation and reflection. Revelation, if it exists, cannot convey any information that is contrary to truth obtained by reason. Note how Locke's perspective on reason differs from Luther's and Aquinas's:

> Traditional Revelation may make us know propositions knowable also by Reason, but not with the same Certainty that Reason doth. Secondly, I say that the same truths may be discovered and conveyed down from revelation, which are discoverable to us by reason, and by those ideas we naturally may have. . . . Revelation cannot be admitted against the clear evidence of Reason. (*Essay* 4, 18, 4-5)

Faith then is useful only to learn things which we cannot discover by our use of reason, such as the fall of angels and the resurrection of the dead. Ironically Locke insisted that the certainty of faith is higher than that of reason, "because the testimony is of such an one as cannot deceive nor be deceived: and that is of God himself. This carries with it assurance beyond doubt, evidence beyond exception" (*Essay* 4, 16, 14). But before revealed information can be accepted as truth, reason must show that it is in fact revealed.

In a later work, *The Reasonableness of Christianity as Delivered in the Scriptures* (1695), Locke argues that reason must be given the last word in the acceptance of the supernatural and the interpretation of Scripture. Most interesting is his insistence that the essence of Christianity is belief in Jesus as God's Messiah sent into the world to spread the true knowledge of God and of our duty. Impressed as he was with the ability of reason to discover all truths necessary to life, and secure in his understanding of morality (remember he shared in the broad and pervasive consensus that assumed without question Christian values), he felt less and less need for revelation. Rationalists, like their medieval predecessors, conceived of revelation as information rather than as God's active making right by his self-revelation. Accepting revelation—believing Christianity—was more a polite compliment paid to God than it was repentance and conversion.

Whether this sort of apologetic influenced people toward or away from Christianity may be debated, but it did call forth reaction on the part of those who viewed Christianity differently. As examples we will look briefly at two apologists whose defense of the faith foreshadowed the cleavage in modern Western consciousness: one turned inward to "reasons of the heart," the other looked outward to find traces of God in his creation.

The first, Blaise Pascal (1623-62), was raised in the atmosphere of Descartes's logical proofs and Montaigne's skepticism. These contributed to the view, similar to Locke's, that matters of faith lay beyond reason. In 1654 Pascal came into contact with a group of evangelical Catholics and was converted and discovered, as he put it, that the God of Abraham, the God of Isaac, the God of Jacob was not that of philosophers and men of science. His religion came to be centered on his personal experience of Christ as Savior and on the wretchedness and nobility of man.

In his influential *Pensées,* which are no more than notes for an apologetic left at his death, he sketches out his approach. Like Augustine, who was such an influence on his thought, he believed that the certainties of faith are attainable only to the heart that loves. Also like Augustine, he believed that man can find his peace only in God. "If man was not made for God, why is he never happy except in God? If man was made for God, why is he so contrary to God?" (Fragment 438). People are fated to choose for or against God, though many go through life caring nothing about this eternal decision. "This same man who spends so many days and nights in rage and despair for the loss of office, or for some imaginary insult to his honour, is the very one who knows without anxiety and without emotion that he will lose all by death." In the light of this, Pascal asks, what really does it mean to be reasonable? He continues:

Nothing reveals more an extreme weakness of mind than not to know the misery of a godless man. Nothing is more indicative of a bad disposition of heart than not to desire the truth of eternal promises. Nothing is more dastardly than to act with bravado before God. . . . Let them recognize that there are two kinds of people one can call reasonable; those who serve God with all their heart because they know Him, and those who seek Him with all their heart because they do not know Him. (Fragment 194)

Clearly Pascal does not despise reason, but man must act. He must decide, and if reason does not help him here, of what use is it? He freely admits that Christianity is beyond our ability to explain. But it is not beyond our ability to choose, and choose we must: "Let us weigh the gain and the loss in wagering that God is. Let us estimate these two chances. If you gain, you gain all; if you lose, you lose nothing. Wager, then, without hesitation that He is" (Fragment 233).

Like Augustine, Pascal insisted that reason's proper office is to aid the heart in submitting to God. "It is the heart which experiences God, and not the reason. This, then, is faith: God felt by the heart, not by the reason" (Fragment 278). Pascal expresses what must be the essential point in his analysis of the relation of faith and reason. Faith is the commitment of the whole person to God; reason is the exercise of that part of man which enables him to make sense of his experience. If the final truth is that God exists and that we were made to know him, then reason best fulfills its role by leading us to understand this. Submission to God does not go against reason but beyond it, just as the whole is beyond the part. In faith, then, "the heart has its reasons, which reason does not know" (Fragment 277).

Several decades later in England, Joseph Butler (1692-1752) conceived an equally famous apologetic that sought confirmation not within the heart but outside in the world. In 1736 appeared his *Analogy of Religion, Natural and Revealed, to the Constitution and*

Course of Nature. Appealing to those who are conscious of order and regularity in nature but who do not believe in orthodox Christianity, Butler makes an analogy between natural phenomena and revealed truth. If we assume that God exists and that he governs the world, "we find by experience . . . that he actually exercises dominion and government over us at present, by rewarding and punishing us for our actions in a strict and proper sense of these words" (1-2, 7). His emphasis on experience shows his dependence on Lockean empiricism, but now he seeks to support Christianity on an entirely new front. Butler attempts to show from human experience that Christianity is credible. If our conclusions cannot be certain, they can be probable. Moreover we need not deny reason the right to judge revelation, for reason is "the only faculty we have wherewith to judge concerning anything, even revelation itself" (2, 3, 2), but the scheme that reason must discern in the world and in revelation is a single program of God. If we refuse to accept God's plan of redemption, Butler seems to argue, we cannot accept the truth of science either. Since we can have only probability in science, we cannot ask for more in revelation. In both reason and revelation there is an element of the incomprehensible, but in the Bible we see much that accords with what we know from experience, such as inequality, rewards and punishments. Moreover the Bible offers us the evidence of prophecy and miracle, which serve to increase the probability for Christianity. And as Butler liked to say, "Probability is the very guide of life."

We appreciate Butler's contribution, for he did more than any other person to stem the tide toward deism, the belief that God created the world but then left it to run autonomously. The *Oxford Dictionary of the Christian Church* comments of the *Analogy*: "In the long run it did more to discredit the movement [of deism] than the vast body of polemical literature, now forgotten, which sought to grapple with its upholders directly." But for all that, Butler's argument leaves the serious reader with lingering doubts. Although it seems impressive as a whole, it often cannot stand up to close examination. Butler frequently responds to objections as if to neutralize an attack were to gain a victory. But the most serious flaw, as J. K. S. Reid notes, is that his argument is dangerously double-edged. "Butler's concept of analogy, so far from winning assurance for the Christian faith, only infects it with the same uncertainty as characterizes knowledge of mundane things" (Reid, p. 153). Butler helped to establish the empirical dimension of apologetics, but his rationalistic framework tends to reduce Christianity to a system of discrete facts that can be expressed in propositional statements. Propositional truth is one important aspect of Christianity, but other areas, such as cultural diversity, historical continuity and personal relevance, are also important. These unexplored areas will occupy apologetics in the modern period.

The Modern Period
The emphasis on rational apologetics had seemed to monopolize apologetic discussion, and a reaction was bound to come. We have seen that an emphasis on reason and knowledge entered the Christian tradition through Greek philosophy, which had emphasized reasoning as a means of salvation. If you know the truth, Greek philosophers had assumed, you will do it. This emphasis is quite different from Christ's: "You will know the truth, and the truth will make you free" (Jn 8:32). In the biblical view, knowledge is a means to life, not the end itself.

In the nineteenth century, Western thinkers began to react against the domination of this Greek tradition in apologetics. We saw earlier that the first Christians emphasized Christian behavior as evidence for Christian truth, and so in a way the reaction against rationalism was a return to an emphasis that had been lost. Like all reactions, this one was prone to excesses. Reason was not only put in its place but sometimes left entirely out of account.

The reaction began with the Danish philosopher Sören Kierkegaard (1813-55). He studied all the rational systems of his day; he passed much of his early life in idleness and amusement; and as he looked about him at the church he saw nothing but churchmanship and politics. His melancholic disposition, physical handicap and disappointment in love all contributed to a reaction against the cold, rational view of Christianity that was current. Rationalism failed, said Kierkegaard, to take account of the most important factor: the individual person. Reflecting Luther's emphasis, he wrote:

Speculation can have nothing to do with sin; in fact, it ought not to have anything to do with sin. Sin belongs to the sphere of ethics; but ethical and speculative thought are moving in opposite directions. The latter abstracts from reality, the former makes for it. Hence it is that ethics operates with a category which speculation ignores and despises—viz. the individual. *(Fear and Trembling)*

It was the individual and the passion directing his or her life that concerned Kierkegaard. What good is it to build a great philosophical system if one must endure a narrow and confined existence? Kierkegaard likened the abstract thinker to a person watching a stage play, all the while glancing at his watch to see if he will miss an appointment. Fool, Kierkegaard would say, you are not merely watching a play; you are on stage and you must act your part. The problems in life cannot be solved by an escape to the world of thought.

Truth for Kierkegaard is a matter of passionate inwardness. For God perhaps truth appears as a system, but for the individual it appears as a paradox. Since God exists in perfect transcendence—otherness from humanity—how can we understand the Incarnation of Christ? This, Kierkegaard insists, is a paradox against which reason beats its head until the blood comes. Truth must be "an objective uncertainty held fast in an appropriation-process of the most passionate inwardness" (1941, p. 182). It can be apprehended only by faith, what he calls a leap, an eternal decision for Christ. It is a passionate decision that transforms the person, and it is a unique experience that cannot be doubted. Do we look for proof for this faith? No indeed; in fact we must regard proof as an enemy. "When faith begins to feel embarrassed and ashamed, like a young woman for whom her love is no longer sufficient, but who secretly feels ashamed of her lover and must therefore have it established that there is something remarkable about him—when faith thus begins to lose its passion, when faith begins to cease to be faith, then a proof becomes necessary so as to command respect from the side of unbelief" (1941, p. 31).

There is much to admire in Kierkegaard: his strong and living conception of God, his understanding of the predicament of the person and his courage to speak against the hypocrisy he saw around him. But one wonders in the end if it is possible to make such a separation between faith and reason. Perhaps he was himself captive to the narrow view of reason the rationalists had fallen into: is it possible for any reasoning process to be purely objective? On the other hand, can any genuinely human faith not have an objective dimension? Augustine had insisted that man's driving passion is toward objective truth, toward God himself.

Furthermore one wonders if Kierkegaard is correct in insisting that the individual is really unique; he seems to make the mistake of today's dogmatic cultural relativists who say that each culture is unique and cannot be judged by any outside standard. If this were true it would be impossible to make any general statement about people or to formulate any generalized theory of culture, and such human studies as psychology, anthropology and sociology would be inconceivable. But in fact man does share characteristics with those around him, and there are objective truths that make understanding possible. The fact that choice and decision are necessary does not keep religion from including objective and historical elements.

Another modern point of view we examine has focused on these objective elements, sometimes to the exclusion of the personal element that Kierkegaard prized. As Kierkegaard is heir to the inwardness of Augustine and Pascal, so these positivists or, more recently, analytic philosophers continue the traditions of British empiricism. Their basic assumption is that all meaningful assertions either are matters of fact subject to scientific verification or are tautological (where the predicate simply reiterates in other words the subject). If Kierkegaard began by assuming the transcendence of God and the consequent limitation of human knowledge, these philosophers assume the reliability of sense experience and thus are suspicious of all claims to transcendent knowledge. According to their *verifiability principle*, the meaning of a proposition is identical with the method of verifying it.

To see how these views challenged Christianity, let us look briefly at positivist A. J. Ayer's classical statement in *Language Truth and Logic*. There he asks what empirical evidence could possibly be marshaled to verify the proposition "God exists." All one can reasonably say is that regularity in nature or certain personal experiences may support this proposition. But religious people, when they argue that God exists, certainly affirm more than that nature is regular in its operations. But how can we describe this reality? One cannot of course show statements about God to be false; they are simply meaningless expressions of personal preference. Statements about transcendent truth simply cannot be verified, Ayer believed, and so they cannot be counted as knowledge. Religious experience is useless as evidence because, says Ayer, "no act of intuition can be said to reveal a truth about any matter of fact unless it issues in verifiable propositions" (p. 120). Religious statements provide material for the psychoanalyst but not for the philosopher.

While many philosophers today work in Ayer's tradition, few would accept his narrow description of meaningful statements. Immediate criticism was leveled at the verifiability principle itself, that no statement can be literally meaningful unless it can be empirically verified. Is it a metaphysical statement or merely a recommendation? If it is the first we have no way of knowing whether it is true, for like statements about God and religion it is unverifiable; if it is the second we cannot tell whether it has any authority. Ayer's friends soon pointed out, moreover, that the principle not only excludes religious truths but also scientific laws which cannot be strictly verified. This criticism led Ayer to formulate a "weak" verification principle which allowed a statement to be meaningful if it could possibly be verified, had some evidential support or could be falsified.

By this time, however, the whole notion of limiting knowledge by scientific criteria was being questioned by scholars within the positivist camp itself, specifically by Ludwig Wittgenstein, who focused on the nature of meaning. Meaning, Wittgenstein now insisted, is a matter of usage, not principle. One cannot decree what can be meaningful; if a statement conforms to the rules of a particular language it must have meaning. If you wish to test empirical statements by actual experience you may, but you may not limit meaning to verifiable statements. It is wrong then either to locate all meaning outside objective truth (as Kierkegaard and his followers tended to do) or to feature objective truth at the expense of personal meaning (as many positivists did). We must find some way to hold the objective and the personal together.

Two additional modern attempts to state Christianity with new relevance conclude our brief sketch, and provide perspectives that we have sensed are missing in a convincing defense of Christianity. Significantly, both come from the Third World where wholly new approaches have come to the defense of Christianity. The first comes from a Japanese who was for many years a missionary in Thailand. In 1974 Kosuke Koyama published *Waterbuffalo Theology*. The importance of his Third-World setting is clear:

> On my way to the country church, I never fail to see a herd of waterbuffaloes grazing in the muddy paddy field. This sight is an inspiring moment for me. Why? Because it reminds me that the people to whom I am to bring the gospel of Christ spend most of their time with these waterbuffaloes in the rice field. The waterbuffaloes tell me that I must preach to these farmers in the simplest sentence-structure and thought development. They remind me to discard all abstract ideas, and to use exclusively objects that are immediately tangible. (p. ix)

His central concern is how to present the Christian faith to people who have no tradition of abstract thinking. The people Koyama describes desire harmony with the cycles of nature and tranquility in their personal relationships. How can they relate, Koyama asks, to a Christianity which says: "In the beginning was the Word"? To a Buddhist monk meditating in his monastery such a view could only be jarring and incomprehensible.

Koyama faces here the challenge that traditional formulations of Christianity often do not communicate in Asia today, where Christianity is seen as a foreign import. Koyama, recalling Kierkegaard, claims that the Western emphasis on history does not speak to the Asian predicament. In the West we experience history through our brains, says Koyama, while the "people there experience history—its hope and despair—with tremendous realism through their famished stomachs" (p. 23). They take history seriously, but in a different, more immediate way that responds less to philosophy than to the good news of a Savior who bore our griefs and carried our sorrows. To a people oriented to the cycles of nature, Koyama wonders, how can a linear view of history be satisfying? He proposes that we think of history as an ascending spiral in which time and nature can be understood together. After all, the regularity of nature is an expression of God's promise: "God's emancipation of man from both dungeon and darkness must be kept in close relationship with the God who desires the regular coming of the monsoon" (p. 37). There must be some way to value what is good in this world view while allowing Christ and the gospel to speak.

For centuries the church has appropriated the insights of its Greco-Roman cultural heritage to express and defend Christianity. This heritage has often served it well. But in recent years there have been signs that certain aspects of the gospel are not being heard and that new approaches might liberate often overlooked elements of the biblical message. Kierkegaard was such a sign of unrest a century and a half ago, and today various non-Western cultural traditions are voicing similar concerns. Is there not something almost biblical about a people who experience life in terms of the cycles of nature and whose thought patterns feature concrete images? Cannot Christianity, Koyama wonders, address itself more directly to people in such a world?

Few would want to argue with Professor Koyama at this point. Yet one wonders whether, if Jesus Christ is the end of history, something final does not happen when the gospel is preached. Koyama wrestles with this question, and we need to hear what he has to say. To the Buddhist principle of detachment, we reply that God has attached himself to this world; to the Eastern idea of tranquility, we respond with the discomfort we feel when we share the sufferings of our crucified Lord. We can only stammer about this noisy attachment of God to the world. "The word which was in the beginning became, in Jesus of Nazareth, the crucified word. The Lord of creation is now the head of the Church. None of us can halt this divine progression! Christ in whom all things hold together is the Christ of whom only the 'Word of the cross' can adequately bear witness" (p. 226).

While we may not agree with Professor Koyama at every point, we can be grateful for his striking formulation of an element all too often missing in apologetics: looking carefully at the setting where the gospel is to penetrate, and speaking the truth in a way that can be heard in that setting. But we must continue to ask of an Asian point of view: Is there no direction to history based on the finished redemptive work of Christ? Perhaps this is one place in Asia the gospel of the kingdom speaks its critical word. Is this not the history we are called upon to fulfill?

These are the questions that our final spokesman, Jose Miguez-Bonino, addresses. As a Latin American from Argentina, Miguez-Bonino is concerned about not only the spiritual aspects of religion but also its concrete and historical reality. In his book *Doing Theology in a Revolutionary Situation* (1975) he explores the idea, shocking to many Western theologians, that Christianity has something to do with political structures. As Christians, he argues, we cannot be indifferent to the concrete historical situation in which we find ourselves; if this situation is repressive to large numbers of people, our faith must respond to the challenge by corporate action.

The challenge to the Christian faith here lies in the fact that to many poor people, Christianity is identified with Western materialism and exploitation. Hunger and repression are serious challenges to Christianity for many people. Communism and other ideologies propose solutions; what does Christianity have to say? Western Christianity seldom has thought in these terms, probably because other challenges such as atheism and evolution have seemed more threatening. But now we are realizing that for vast segments of the human family practical questions are more pressing than philosophical ones. For these, says Miguez-Bonino, truth must be shown in terms of concrete political action rather than only in abstract thinking. This is not unbiblical: scriptural ideas grow out of particular situations through which and in terms of which God revealed himself. "The meaning of Christianity cannot be abstracted from its historical significance" (p. 92). The word is demonstrated and verified in the act; therefore as we obey in the concrete place where God has put us, we will grow in understanding. Scripture demands an ethical response, as the book of James makes clear.

The most striking aspect of Miguez-Bonino's view is his assertion that secular and sacred history are one:

> There is scarcely a question of "two histories" in relation to the Old Testament. There, God's action takes place in history and as history. It inextricably involves human action and, conversely, there is no human action reported outside the relation with God's purpose and word. (p. 134)

Contrary to Augustine's conception of history as the interaction between two cities, which Miguez-Bonino believes reduces actions to no more than their individual significance, he insists that there is only one level of significance: that in which God builds his church. "The kingdom is not the denial of history but the elimination of its corruptibility . . . in order to bring to full realization the true meaning of the communal life of man" (p. 142). God is filling history with his purposes, and we are called upon to work toward their realization. This we do, knowing that all our work in proclaiming and living the gospel will be fulfilled when God intervenes to bring history to a close.

This new perspective in apologetics insists that all human actions individually and corporately belong to a higher order. Christianity is not reduced to pointing to the future; it claims validity for its present vocation. Here however we must be cautious. Miguez-Bonino and others have helped us see the immanence of God in history and the necessity of historical obedience. While this emphasis is helpful, it risks overlooking the transcendent dimensions of God's purposes and restricting the kingdom to particular social or political programs. We do not seek support for Christianity in the newspaper or the history book; rather we present Christianity as the validation of all human activities.

Christianity may well seem foreign in many parts of the world because it is presented as a system of ideas to which only a Westerner can relate. Perhaps non-Western mentalities would understand more readily the idea of a power confrontation. We shall have more to say about this further on; suffice it to suggest at this point that Miguez-Bonino may well be reminding us of a dimension often missing from our apologetic, one that the early church understood well: Faith must have a visible reality, and the gospel must be presented as the power of God unto salvation. But we must not forget that Christianity finds its essence in particular events wherein God was reconciling the world unto himself, and that these events and their explanation are found in Scripture, which must always be normative for faith and practice. This is God's way of making his will known in a fallen world. Moreover the West may make a unique contribution by insisting that defense of the Christian faith is not ad hoc response to daily needs or miscellaneous reflections on cultural diversity, but a careful, consistent presentation of the structure of God's program.

We will next suggest an apologetic approach that seeks to combine all these diverse elements in a defense for Christianity: those factual elements that all mankind must deal with and which belong to the givens of our world; those elements of reason and logic which help us make a whole of our disparate experiences; and finally those personal and cultural elements that make us all what we are and which we must express in any genuine religious commitment.

Questions for Review

1. What three challenges did the apostles face?
2. How would you characterize Origen's defense in *Contra Celsus?*
3. Name at least two of Augustine's contributions to the history of apologetics.
4. Contrast Anselm's and Aquinas's use of reason in their apologetics.
5. What characterized apologetics during the Reformation?
6. In what ways did rationalism grow out of the Reformation?
7. What role does reason play in the thought of Pascal? Of Locke?
8. What were the strengths and weaknesses of Butler's *Analogy of Religion?*
9. How did Kierkegaard react against the emphasis on reason?
10. Koyama tries to explain Christianity in relation to the hearer's cultural context. What are the dangers of such an attempt?
11. In Miguez-Bonino's response to his situation, what is his conception of history?
12. Name at least one contribution each tradition represented in this chapter—Greek, Latin-American and Asian—could make to our understanding of apologetics.

Major Project: Trace Christian understanding of the relation between faith and reason through all the periods of Christian history.

CHAPTER THREE

Elements of Apologetic Argument

W——————————

e have discerned three very different challenges to Christianity which we shall separate and treat individually. First, does Christianity fit the facts? Does the world we live in, its nature and its history, corroborate the claims that Christians make about God and his purposes? Since we claim that God is the creator and sustainer of the world, his presence should become evident by a careful assessment of what is there. The challenge coming from Latin America forces us to ask: can history be read only in terms of Christianity or does some alternative, such as Marxism, make more sense?

Second, does Christianity make sense? Is it a consistent system in which all parts logically and naturally fit together? There must be structure and wholeness to a way of looking at things that "makes sense." In general, Westerners have concentrated on this rationalistic aspect of apologetics, sometimes to the exclusion of other approaches, so we shall look to Western traditions for help in systematically analyzing the Christian faith.

Third, does Christianity matter? Is it personally and culturally relevant? We may agree that certain facts point to the truth of Christianity; we may accept certain lines of reasoning; and still we may feel that Christianity is too remote and distant. Asians often perceive Christianity as a foreign product. In China, for example, many have observed that Christianity has failed to make a lasting impact; it has never penetrated into Chinese culture, whereas Buddhism, also a foreign import, quickly took on Chinese characteristics and is now considered a native Chinese religion. Why did this not happen to Christianity? How can Christianity, with all its arguments and facts, be made relevant to the millions of Third-World people who live on the verge of starvation? Christianity must be brought a good deal closer to where people live, both individually and communally, before it will win response and commitment. This has been recognized by some Westerners ever since Kierkegaard made a philosophical place for the individual. Thus we will look to Western existentialists along with Asian thinkers as we face this third challenge to the Christian faith.

We believe Christianity can well meet each of these three challenges. The case for faith in Christ appears much stronger when all types of argumentation are used. Let us examine each challenge in turn.

Does Christianity Fit the Facts?

This way of arguing for Christianity fits into the general philosophical tradition of empiricism. Stemming from the Greek philosopher Aristotle, it has had famous Christian exponents such as Thomas Aquinas, Joseph Butler and William Paley. While not denying logical reasoning, these thinkers insist that rationalistic explanations are insufficient. The world does not always fit into neat, logical categories. As Mary B. Hesse has quipped: "A clear understanding of the relativity of logic and mathematics is a great gain, since we require a healthy distrust of logic when it is applied to the real world" (p. 88). And since the real world is where most people live, we must develop dimensions of reasoning beyond the mathematical or logical; we must also use inductive or historical reasoning. Empirical argument may not give us the neat certainty that we would like, but it can give us probability. This way of thinking must recognize that new discoveries may invalidate old hypotheses. But it has the advantage of appealing to data that is public, that everyone can examine and that cannot be dismissed as a product of religious imagination.

This approach to Christian defense includes the area called *natural theology*, the study of truths about Christianity or God that can be known apart from special revelation. It looks at the world to find evidence for the truth of Christianity. It is an approach used by theists to argue for the existence of God as well as by Christians to defend their unique view of God and salvation. We shall, in fact, study theistic arguments before turning to a specifically Christian approach, since theism, while not sufficient in itself to prove the truth of Christianity, is certainly a necessary foundation for any convincing argument.

We begin with our objective setting, because we are creatures of space and time who cannot think or know anything except in terms of objects and events. These all may become signs and pathways by which God comes to us. Before the Fall Adam and Eve could speak directly with God; now he must come to us, as Luther said, veiled in the signs of his love and presence. Are there such signs? Let us see.

The natural order. Perhaps the most famous exponent of the empirical argument for theism is Cambridge philosopher F. R. Tennant (1866-1957; see Ramm, 1965, pp. 125-44). Tennant denied any possibility of religious knowledge except through the senses. Reason cannot function apart from sense experience, he maintained, and even the most profound religious experience is open to doubt; it cannot in itself prove that God exists. Nor can we base our faith on revelation alone. Just because it comes from "out there" does not mean God is its source. We must be able to test all religious belief in some public way. We cannot ask people to put faith in something that cannot be reasonably demonstrated by experience.

Tennant begins with the experience of everyday life, what he calls *presumptive knowledge*. From this raw data, he believes, ethics and religion can be abstracted; every perception has the promise of thought when it is clarified and explained. This process of clarification leads us from presumptive knowledge to larger and larger laws and hypotheses which account for the data of our experience. Tennant called this process "epigenesis."

As philosophers we are not only interested in our own experience, but in the experience of the whole human race, the whole world. According to Tennant, epigenesis is the only way to ground or support statements about God or the world. Thus we are driven by faith—the ineradicable effort of the will to carry verification to its conclusion—to suggest hypotheses that go beyond the data of our experience in order to account ultimately for that experience. In this way we seek to understand the person, for example, with the category of personality, which Tennant calls "our highest interpretive concept. For the theist, it is the key to the universe" (1928, 1:127). Since we know of human personality, we can suggest the existence of a personal God as a hypothesis building on and going beyond the hypotheses of science.

We can see by looking at two doctrines how this method works. Take the doctrine of the soul, basic to all religions. A person's consciousness of the external world leads to self-consciousness. This awareness of being aware is the basic reality for human beings. It accompanies all our experiences of external reality; we cannot deny it without confusion. Moreover we are aware of a unity of personal life which we call "I." For Tennant, the existence of the soul is the only satisfactory way to account for a person's continuity through time and for the individuality of his or her experience.

How can we establish the existence of God? Tennant bases his argument here on the "conspiration of innumerable causes to produce, by their united and reciprocal action, and to maintain, a general order of nature" (1928, 2:9). This order, which he calls "cosmic teleology," cannot be explained by chance. "The multitude of interwoven adaptations by which the world is constituted a theatre of life, intelligence, and morality, cannot reasonably be regarded as an outcome of mechanism, or of blind formative power, or of ought but purposive intelligence" (1928, 2:121). Tennant believes he is doing here only what the scientist does all the time, forming hypotheses by alogical probability. The theologian takes up the argument just where the scientist leaves off.

> All causal science is, in the last resort, but reasonable and postulatory, teleology is therefore a continuation, by extrapolation, of the plotted curve which comprehensively describes its knowledge. And this is the *apologia* for theism such as professes to be reasonable belief for the guidance of life, when arranged by science and logic or by more pretentious theology. (1928, 2:120)

In his semi-popular book *The Nature of Belief,* Tennant adds another element worth noting: he argues that faith can be pragmatically verified. Just as the truth of a scientific hypothesis is verified by appeal to external facts, so faith is verified by its fruitfulness in practical life. Though he thinks this defense will satisfy many people, it is dangerous. As he himself admits, "The fruitfulness of a belief is one thing, and the reality or existence of what is ideated and assumed is another" (1943, pp. 70-71).

We may admire the daring and scope of this line of reasoning and yet register misgivings: one must be careful what sort of foundation is laid for Christianity. Tennant in one place maintains that only in science do we have "indisputable facts." On the basis of scientific certainty, he argues, we can project the superstructure of belief in God. One might well question whether science does in fact give us an adequate foundation. First, over the last hundred years, scientific revolutions have taken place in several branches of science. What has appeared certain to one generation has appeared not certain at all to the next. Second, scientific data and hypotheses are nonreligious data, and some critics of Tennant have asked how we can draw religious conclusions from nonreligious information. Religious experience has at least the merit of being intrinsically religious in character; it is an encounter with God that is claimed. Finally, Tennant might not have dismissed revelation so quickly had he remembered that it is not only the voice of God from the mountain but also his involvement in human history. It is to this history that we now turn.

The witness of history. If God is truly the creator and sustainer of the world, we will likely see signs of his presence in history. It is natural for us to seek him in events, because we are creatures whose lives consist in a series of interconnected happenings. Austin Farrer says: "Remove the knowledge of historical facts and there is no field left in which revelation can appear" (p. 52).

For an historically based apologetic argument we look at J. W. Montgomery's *The Shape of the Past.* Montgomery, an American evangelical theologian, agrees with Tennant that we cannot make Christianity rest on "values inaccessible to science." Therefore we must reject any method that rests on subjective experience, pragmatism or papal supremacy. Rather we must seek to ground Christianity on indisputable historical truths, in particular the resurrection of Jesus Christ from the dead.

Let us see how this historical method works. Two things are necessary for the honest historian: suspension of disbelief and examination of the evidence. In other words historians must not make up their minds in advance what they will see but must face the facts as they are. Now the Gospel records, says Montgomery, are reliable and trustworthy documents about Christ's life. In these records Jesus makes divine claims and exercises divine prerogatives. We cannot escape the conclusion that he claimed to be God in the form of a man. The Gospels all record his resurrection in minute detail, and this resurrection is convincing evidence for his deity (unless, Montgomery notes, you rule out resurrection a priori and insist that resurrections cannot happen). If Jesus is God, then all that he said about the Old Testament, man and sin must be true. By extension, all biblical assertions bearing on the philosophy of history are considered true because God is their source.

Montgomery makes two qualifications to his line of thinking.

First, it is true that the resurrection can be established only as probable, but probability is all that can be required of any historical argument. If we did not accept probability in historical judgments, we would disbelieve not only Christianity but all other historical assertions as well. Here Montgomery makes an important contribution to apologetic argument: it is inadmissible to ask more of a line of reasoning than it can possibly give. Historical judgments are based on available records. No historical data can ever be conclusive. In historical reasoning, therefore, we can expect only probability, and we must not be disappointed when we cannot have certainty. The uncertainty here is not with Christianity, but with the tenuous nature of historical argumentation.

Montgomery's second qualification is that we cannot expect historical argument to force anyone to become a Christian. Each person must choose freely to believe or disbelieve. But historical evidence does give solid objective ground for testing the Christian faith experientially. Such a test, Montgomery concludes, will show that the Christian faith is ultimately self-validating. He does not insist that this argument be used in isolation from other approaches but that it be the primary rational support that we ask of Christian truth.

Much in Montgomery's approach is valuable. Christianity is based on historical events that must be subject to historical investigation. God did not bring about salvation in a secret place but in the full glare of public scrutiny. Thus historical evidences must always play an important role in our defense. But, as Montgomery himself recognizes, this line of defense is not sufficient by itself. Its limitations lie in two general areas: it is limited in scope and insufficient in force.

These objections were anticipated two hundred years ago by G. Lessing, the famous Enlightenment philosopher. Lessing admits that he can raise no important historical objection to the resurrection of Christ, or to the claim that his disciples declared him the Son of God. But he argues:

If on historical grounds I have no objection to the statement

that Christ raised to life a dead man; must I therefore accept it
as true that God has a son that is of the same essence as himself?
. . . But to jump with that historical truth to a quite different
class of truths, and to demand of me that I should form all my
metaphysical and moral ideas accordingly, if that is not a trans-
fer to another genus, then I do not know what Aristotle meant
by this phrase. (pp. 54-55)

Lessing is saying here that the bare fact of the resurrection, even
assuming it is true, is not enough to establish the truth of Christianity: first, because it does not in itself prove other truths which
belong to the Christian faith—for example, that God has a Son;
second, because it does not require me to do anything in particular that might be called Christian—such as change all my
moral ideas. Lessing is not denying that the resurrection might
provide partial support for these things, but he is pointing out the
limitation of such historical reasoning. This is an observation we
may elaborate a bit more.

The historical approach is also central, and let us look more closely at the limitation in scope of the historical approach. Although the resurrection of Christ is central,
it does not stand alone, nor is it the only element of Christian
truth subject to historical investigation. Christ in fact came to
fulfill Old Testament promises, and thus he cannot be isolated
from these promises. Biblical revelation—the Old Testament
people of Israel, the person and work of Christ, and the founding
of the Christian church—makes a whole that transcends the sum
of its parts. So to historical facts we need to add rational arguments to make Christian reality convincing. We need, in short,
an interpretation of historical facts.

The historical approach is also insufficient in force: I can always say to historical evidence, So what? What does this have to
do with me? Until I see myself as a sinner standing in danger of
the wrath of God, I will not understand the importance of the
facts of Christ's life. Moreover I cannot approach data objectively
because my perception is distorted by sin and prejudice. So the
facts of Christ's life need to be presented, as Romans 1:16 says, as
"the power of God for salvation," not merely as interesting an-

cient happenings. Thus historical argumentation needs to be supplemented by personal and existential factors including the witness and illumination of the Holy Spirit.

Does Christianity Make Sense?

The problem with facts, we have suggested, is that they don't tell us enough. Facts need to be interpreted; they need to be put in a framework in which they can be understood. Creating such a framework involves reasoning which starts from certain ideas (sometimes called axioms or presuppositions) and draws consistent conclusions.

Some think that a reasoned defense of Christianity is an academic exercise deriving from Greek philosophy and irrelevant to real life. Before drawing such a far-reaching conclusion, we need to consider several things. First, Christians believe that the created order of the world, though fallen, reflects the consistent character of God. The Scriptures imply that we can still depend on the general providence of God: the rain comes and the sun shines from day to day. We can deny this order if we wish—we can deny gravity and jump from a four-story building—but we will suffer the consequences. Second, both Scripture and the social sciences indicate that the structure of human thinking reflects (as well as shapes) the order of God's creation. Moreover Christians believe that human capacity to think and reason reflects God's own thinking. As he is transcendent over the world and can understand and direct its processes, so we in our human way can transcend our situation, make symbols of it, and so understand and control it. This ability is a human—not only a Greek —characteristic. Third, though each people will not reason in the same way, there are certain basic ways of approaching the world that transcend cultural or personal differences. We are ultimately one race; we live in a unified created structure. Therefore we put together what is similar (that is, we use analogy); we separate what is different (that is, we use the law of noncontradiction); and we conclude that if something proves true for us it will do the same for others (that is, we make inferences from what we know is true). Thus reasoning is not merely an academic exercise: it is based on the consistency of God's purposes and reflects the goodness of his created order. As creatures of a God who understands, we seek coherence in our knowing.

It is true that in the West rational principles often become ultimates requiring final commitment. Immanuel Kant, for example, was prepared to doubt anything except the rational structure of his mind. Even God he subordinated to these principles. This point of view, called *rationalism*, appears all too frequently. But it should not blind us to the fact that rationality is a gift of God and can be used like any other gift in his service. Let us now examine some thinkers who have argued along this line.

Perhaps the most famous evangelical apologist who has developed a rational defense is the American Calvinist Cornelius Van Til, retired professor at Westminster Seminary. His starting point is the fundamental distinction between God's knowledge and human knowledge. Only God has true knowledge of the world as it really exists; thus only he can give us true knowledge of the world. If we try to know the world apart from God we will misunderstand it, because we are sinners and sin has affected our ability to think. Perhaps before the Fall Adam and Eve had a clear intuitive understanding of the world. Now every time a person tries to know something apart from God, he distorts it. To know anything truly, therefore, we must presuppose that the God speaking in the Bible is the true God. Van Til makes this point clearly:

Every form of intellectual argument rests, in the last analysis, upon one or the other of two basic presuppositions. The non-Christian's process of reasoning rests upon the presupposition that man is the final or ultimate reference point in human predication. The Christian's process of reasoning rests upon the presupposition that God, speaking through Christ by his Spirit in the infallible Word, is the final or ultimate reference point in human predication. (1963, p. 180)

This point of view, far from denying reason a place, makes it all the more important, for once we assume that God exists and that his Word is true, we have a basis from which reasoning can truly proceed. We can reasonably show that the Christian point of view is coherent and that alternatives are finally incoherent. But it is clear that "the only possible way for the Christian to reason with the non-believer is by way of presupposition. He must say to the unbeliever that unless he will accept the presuppositions and with them the interpretations of Christianity there is no coherence in human experience" (p. 150). Since we cannot reason on the basis of common ground (when the evolutionist and the Christian refer to a tree, for example, they are not even talking about the same reality; for one the tree is a product of evolution, for the other it is created by God and reflects his creative purposes), the best apologetic, Van Til concludes, is a consistent and loving proclamation of the gospel that the Holy Spirit can use to convict of sin and bring to insight.

Van Til's influence on Christian apologetics has been considerable. Much in his approach is useful. He makes it clear that facts cannot be understood outside of some framework. He helps us see that the Creator is a part of his creation, for apart from him it would neither exist nor be what it is. Nevertheless, it is the *fact* of God's existence, not our knowledge of it, that makes the world intelligible. God is the origin of the world's structure even if people do not recognize the fact, and the order that is intrinsic to creation does not go away when God is not acknowledged as its source. So we cannot agree completely with Van Til that there is no common basis for discussion between the Christian and the non-Christian. Van Til insists that "reason employed by a Christian always comes to other conclusions than reason employed by a non-Christian." It is hard to see exactly what this can mean. It is obviously untrue that a non-Christian speaks only falsehood or that a Christian speaks only truth. Of course if each were perfectly consistent with his or her assumptions, we might believe that Christians and non-Christians would always come to different conclusions, and it is precisely this consistency that we must strive to reach. Yet though Scripture assists our thinking, we cannot claim infallibility for our extrapolations from it, for—as we will see in the next section—these are always conditioned by our history and our unique values. Unfortunately this claim to infallibility is often made, and among evangelicals it has led to a damaging dogmatism.

For Van Til, reasoning processes based on Christian presuppositions are sufficient means to truth. For other Christian apologists in his tradition, reason provides a starting point but is not all-sufficient. Let us look at an evangelical theologian who has sought a broader understanding of Christian reasoning. Edward John Carnell, late professor of apologetics at Fuller Seminary, insisted that knowing was more than a mathematical type of inference. In fact there are three ways we know: by immediate acquaintance or experience *(ontological truth)*, by inference from this experience *(propositional truth)*, and by being placed in a moral and spiritual environment *(knowledge of imperative essence)*. On the basis of this third way of knowing he sought to point out a new apologetic approach (see 1957).

In certain situations, Carnell observes, we sense an obligation placed on us and know intuitively that a response is called for. All men and women must act, and actions betray convictions. Carnell notes: "Moral self-acceptance is the method by which these convictions are measured" (1957, p. 38). We call our morality the choices that we make, and those things that express the necessities both of our convictions and of the spiritual environment. But our decisions must reflect intellectual judgment and not only moral feeling. Proper response, that which reflects a worthy faith, can be made only by cooperation between the nature of the object and the sufficiency of the evidence. The very fact that we have judicial sentiments ("that was wrong"; "this is unjust") implies a standard of judgment. Judgment implies an administrator of justice. So God must exist to make the moral cycle meaningful. Concludes Carnell: "Since man is made in the image of God, man shares in the life of God whenever he makes contact with ultimate elements in [the] . . . moral and spiritual environment" (1957, p. 135).

Carnell thus broadens the defense of Christianity: while seeing the importance of traditional reasoning and propositional truth, he points out as well the importance of our value judgments to our understanding the world. Furthermore, he says, in all areas of human endeavor the Christian value judgment is the most consistent. He assumes that a consistent system is a true system. Life as it is lived has its own "logic" that forces certain choices upon us. Although this is a helpful evaluation, two comments about Carnell's approach may be made. First, while the Christian view is a consistent explanation for our response to certain experiences, it may not be the only one. We will note below this weakness of a rational approach to Christianity: rational arguments are sometimes double-edged swords that can be used to argue for the truth of Christianity and also against it. Second, rationality needs to be empirically grounded on the one hand and made personally relevant on the other. It is in this second direction that Carnell is moving, and his moral argument anticipates some of the things we will say in the next section. But before we turn to this let us summarize and evaluate what we have discovered in this second section.

We have seen that bare facts considered outside some framework—even if they are historically grounded—do not help us find truth. If God is the Creator, then history and nature will speak of him, but if his final purposes lie outside this order (for example in his own glory), then we will not understand him or his creation without an explanation that we cannot get from the world. This explanation we believe is found in God's self-revelation in Scripture. Scripture tells us that certain historical events are pivotal in God's eternal purposes, and that understanding his purposes is vital to understanding creation. These scriptural truths then can become foundational (or structural) principles in terms of which we elaborate our knowledge. By comparison and contrast we can apply these truths to the world; we can "reason" in the light of them and discover further truth.

But since these basic explanations relate to historical events which Scripture interprets and not to abstract truths, we will argue below that what we need is not a logical system but an historical one. Thus we will use scriptural truths not like mathematical axioms but like synoptic categories to help us see our experience as a whole in light of God's purposes. After all some of the most important elements of the Christian system are still in the future: the return of Christ and the new heaven and earth. Thus our understanding will have to be open to future revelation of truth, which, we believe, will enrich and expand what we already know to be true.

One final reminder of the limitations of rationality: an argument is only as strong as its premises. If I leave God out, I can argue persuasively, as David Hume did, that miracles are impossible. If however I believe God exists, miracles are perfectly reasonable. Both views are consistent with their premises, for as Michael Polanyi points out, coherence relates only to the stability of a framework which could equally stabilize an erroneous view (p. 294). The Christian view is coherent, but to establish its truth, we must investigate its premises both historically and experientially. Reason alone establishes only the possibility, not the certainty, of truth.

Does Christianity Matter?

E. J. Carnell is one of many modern theologians and philosophers who recognize that experience is vital to knowing. Perhaps Kierkegaard went too far in asserting that traditional rules of logic have no ontological significance: the logical process is not totally unrelated to our experience in the world. But modern philosophy, having received this shock from existentialism, has re-examined human knowledge and discovered that the rules of logic, at least in their traditional form, do not exhaust the meaning of truth. Criteria for truth can be informal as well as formal. Kierkegaard for example pointed out the value of decision in knowledge, insisting that truth has a subjective dimension. Although modern theology has sometimes exaggerated subjectivity, we now know that it cannot be ignored. In the end historical facts and logical rules must be assimilated into and validated by the lived world; conclusive evidence is always experiential. Scripture is clear both that Christianity involves doctrine and that it is a way of living that verifies the truth of doctrine. So we are fully justified in seeking "arguments from experience" growing out of our actual life in the world.

As Carnell observed, there comes a time in any examination of truth claims when a person must ask, "Who am I and what am I to do?" Without leaving reason and facts behind, he or she must decide between Christianity and some other way of life. For involvement and commitment are not unique to Christianity but are required of every human truth claim. To the question "What is truth?" must always be added "What will I do?" The need for commitment is evident in the nature of verification. Religion cannot be verified in some general or abstract way if it is to be true to its own nature; verification of religion must in the nature of the case be a personal realization. It does no good to complain that Christianity is "subjective" when the personal element is indispensable in every religious experience.

Is Christianity relevant to people in real life situations? We will approach the matter from two perspectives: first individually, then corporately in terms of the larger culture.

Individual relevance. First, responsible knowledge demands an appropriate response. Truth when it is understood carries with it certain obligations and responsibilities. If I know that a tornado is bearing down on my town, I must not only believe the report but also see to it that I and those around me move out of danger.

Second, a decision made on the basis of knowledge received not only must be true to the evidence but also must express truly the desires and values of myself and my community. We are all the results of decisions that we have made in the past. We have created our lives in and through our choices. We speak of "sincere" decisions to reform our lives; by this we mean that these decisions honestly express our sense of need and our character. Religious decision is an experience of the whole person. A responsible decision for Christ must be a total commitment of all we are, as we are immersed in the fabric of our lives. Scripture tells us that the Holy Spirit must awaken the sense of need and helplessness that motivates us to turn to Christ.

Here we meet again our basic premise: in religious commitment, faith is the prior category to knowledge. Although knowledge is always involved, our commitment to the truth of the gospel is what finally verifies for us the reality that is there: plugging the cord in the outlet is what finally verifies the reality of the electrical current. Faith is not a general persuasion of truth but the trust and commitment growing out of (and into) such persuasion. As we commit ourselves to Christ, we make real by the Holy Spirit the truth of Christ's death and resurrection. Since we are created in the image of God, we believe moreover that it is only the impact of God's revelation in Christ that makes us fully human.

Now if authentic Christianity is experiential as well as reasonable, I should see evidence for its truth both in my own life and in that of the Christian community. Does such evidence exist? I believe so. (See Green, 84-89.)

First, Christian experience is universally claimed to be based on the historical and exalted Christ. That all Christian testimony agrees on this point gives prima facie evidence for the existence and reality of such a figure. One would have to deny the reality of all these experiences with their consistent testimony to cast doubt on the reality of Christ. Even an unbeliever like James Frazer says in *The Golden Bough:* "The origin of a great moral and religious reform is incredible without the personal existence of a great reformer."

Moreover, similarity of Christian testimony increases its weight as evidence. Christian experience always centers around personal communion with the Savior, claimed by Christians to be the Son of God. In court, witnesses gain credence to the degree that their testimony agrees. Thus the believability of Christian testimony becomes stronger because of this agreement.

Of course it is possible that this experience of Christ is a delusion. Christians may honestly feel they are experiencing what in fact cannot be experienced. But clinical evidence suggests that behavior consistently based on a delusion has a disintegrative effect on the personality (Green, p. 87). Christianity, however, more often than not has a positive moral and spiritual effect on the believer. Fear of death usually displaces false hopes or illusions, but Christians have a firm foundation on which to face death's horrors. Christians claim that Christ helps make men and women whole, and there is evidence to support this claim.

Cultural relevance. Francis Schaeffer pioneered an approach which has been called cultural apologetics. In his book *The God Who Is There,* he argues that by examining modern cultures we can see that loss of faith in God breaks down cultural values and leads to dehumanization.

Schaeffer's method is to examine the view of the person evident in the art and literature of a culture. To uncover the dilemma of the person in any culture, he believes we must evaluate its cultural forms. In the West, tracing the decline of faith in God, one can show how unbelief leads to human disorientation: we see this on every hand in modern art and literature. And yet since we are created for God and cannot live without him, we refuse to believe life is meaningless; we insist on committing ourselves to causes, falling in love, and creating grand symbols of our quests in art and literature. In this attempt to create meaning, Schaeffer claims, we are being inconsistent. We are living off Christian values, even as we deny their source. To approach such people we must point out their inconsistency; as Schaeffer often says, we must "take the roof off" people and show them where they really live. When they see that apart from God none of their pursuits has any meaning (Schaeffer shows his dependence on Van Til at this point), we can present the gospel to them.

Schaeffer has greatly influenced Western Christians, and God has used his books (he has written more than twenty) in two ways. First, by "speaking the gospel into the twentieth century," Schaeffer has often gained a hearing for it among people who would not otherwise listen. Seeing the gospel in terms of their own drives and interests, many have found it relevant and have come to Christ. Second, Schaeffer has made Christians aware of the cultural dimension to faith. Thanks to his writings, many have been encouraged to involve themselves in their culture as salt and light. Here he has performed a great service for the church (and greatly influenced the author of this book). There is no substitute for listening carefully to culture, getting close enough to it to hear its cries and sobs and to feel its unexpressed yearnings. This involvement gives loving our neighbor a vital new dimension.

Yet Schaeffer's cultural apologetics is less applicable in societies where art and literature are not highly developed and which are not post-Christian in outlook. In such places also we need to be culturally sensitive, but we will have to look in different places to see the problems. For example, in Asia today we need to study urbanization, overpopulation and malnutrition, to ask ourselves what Christianity has to say about these problems.

Another limitation of Schaeffer's approach is that it focuses on those elements of culture that fail to express Christian values. Yet every culture contains not only elements which contradict the truth of God but also elements which support that truth. Could we approach culture from the other direction? Could we ask what in my culture supports the truth of Christianity? Don Richardson, working among the Sawi people of Netherlands New Guinea, attempted such a positive approach. After a great deal of initial difficulty making the gospel understandable to these people, he struck on their concept of *peace child*. "Among the Sawi, every demonstration of friendship was suspect except one. If a man would actually give his own son to his enemies, that man could be trusted! That, and that alone, was a proof of goodwill no shadow of cynicism could discredit" (p. 206). Richardson presented Jesus Christ as God's peace child who proves that God can be trusted and that friendship now exists between him and his creation.

Richardson suggests that in every culture—because of our creation in God's image—"redemptive analogies" can be used to demonstrate the truth of Christianity. Surely this approach needs further exploration; it promises to lend strong support to an apologetic responsive to everyday needs.

Excursus: Theistic Argumentation

Since the truth of Christianity presupposes the existence of God, we need to find a way to argue for his existence. Any such argument will need to have several components which appeal to several kinds of reasoning. Let us examine various approaches.

For centuries Western Christians have used the traditional arguments for the existence of God: I have the idea of a perfect being, therefore this being must exist (Anselm); I know of causes, therefore a first cause must exist (Aquinas); created reality acts toward an end, therefore there must be a final purpose (Tennant); and I have a sense of morality, therefore an absolute lawgiver exists (Carnell). While for some people these arguments carry weight, many feel that the God we can prove, even though our arguments may be correct as far as they go, bears little resemblance to the Christian God. This traditional approach emphasizes the cognitive and logical (our second apologetic element), but it neglects other dimensions. As we have already noted, for many people such arguments are not only unconvincing but also unnecessary. When judged by biblical standards, moreover, they are found incomplete. Our awareness of God must be more immediate, and so these arguments may be corroborative but they are rarely sufficient to produce certainty.

A changing understanding of the relation between faith and reason has persuaded many that in arguing for God's existence, we should use many kinds of formal and nonformal reasoning. Previously it was thought that faith related to the volitional part of the person and reason to the cognitive. Now we understand that these functions are far more interrelated than we had thought (see Gill). We can understand faith as an act of rational choice by which we interpret experience. We can see reason involving nonrational assumptions and precommitment. John Hick (1957) has described faith as a stage on the way to final verification. Faith is not a commitment to another realm lying behind and beyond the human so much as an interpretation of the natural world in terms of a divine reality believed to penetrate it. He illustrates this by imagining reality as three interpenetrating "situations" which we interpret in three ways (pp. 106-26). First and most basic is the natural level. We relate ourselves to this level by learning its laws and following their direction. Second is the human situation wherein we are responsible agents subject to moral obligation. This second dimension must be realized in terms of the first. Third is the level of the presence of God, the comprehensive and awesome realization that we live within the sphere of his ongoing purposes. Again we experience this in terms of (not apart from) our experience of the first two situations. Our awareness of the final level is not merely the conclusion of an argument, but the apprehension of divine presence within our natural and moral existence. Since this apprehension is a response of the whole person and not just of the mind, it can be recommended but not argued for in a definitive way.

This is not to say there can be no verification. Hick argues that final verification is possible but only at the end of history when we stand in the presence of God. To illustrate this he tells a story:

Two men are traveling together along a road. One of them believes that it leads to a Celestial City, the other that it leads nowhere; but since this is the only road there is, both must travel it. Neither has been this way before and therefore neither is able to say what they will find around each next corner. During their journey they meet both with moments of refreshment and delight, and with moments of hardship and danger. All the time one of them thinks of his journey as a pilgrimage to a Celestial City and interprets the pleasant parts as encouragements and the obstacles as trials of his purpose and lessons in endurance, prepared by the king of that city and designed to make of him a worthy citizen of the place when at last he arrives there. The other, however, believes none of this and sees their journey as an unavoidable and aimless ramble. Since he has no choice in the matter, he enjoys the good and endures the bad. But for him there is no Celestial City to be reached, no all-encompassing purpose ordaining their journey—only the road itself and the luck of the road in good weather and in bad. (p. 177)

Notice that not only the believer makes a faith decision about the road he is traveling: both men must do so. One, however, has faith in the final purpose; the other believes in the final purposelessness of the way. It is important to see that the faith of the travelers determines how they will view the whole—how they will interpret good times and bad. We differ from Hick in seeing verification not only as future but also, in part, as present reality. For, Scripture insists, we are already the sons and daughters of God (1 Jn 3:2); the delights of knowing the Lord are not only encouragements but also part of the final Christian reality.

Hick argues that a faith commitment is no different from other kinds of decisions we are forced to make. We often live with less than logical certainty. The Oxford philosopher Basil Mitchell pursues this idea. After showing that God's existence can finally be neither disproved nor proved in the usual sense, he argues that we can build a cumulative case for Christianity in the same way that we can argue for any other comprehensive paradigm. We may consider any complex hypothesis certain and act as if it is true, and at the same time feel the need to justify our claim. Mitchell gives the example of liberal democracy (p. 122): he votes and supports this system even while adducing evidence in its support and seeing problems needing attention at this or that point. Living demands such involvement and choice; one cannot wait until all the evidence is in before acting. A religious choice can be this kind of involvement.

Not that there is no evidence. Mitchell argues that a cumulative case can make large theories appear plausible. That there are many claims to revelation does not mean that no claims are true. Intelligent claims can be made; thinking people can evaluate them and commit themselves to them. Moreover, rival systems of interpretation can be compared for their adequacy and consistency. That mystery is present in Christianity is no cause to reject the system: its presence can be accounted for by human sin and divine transcendence. Thus Christians contend that "there are truths which men could not have discovered by themselves, but which God has found means of communicating to them" (p. 156).

Commitment, moral decision and action—which life itself calls for—demand unconditional acceptance of a system of truths which may in themselves be only highly probable. But in the nature of the case such a system can only be made to appear plausible. It might be argued that the Christian seeks (and the Bible promises) certainty about the promises of God. This we believe we can have, but not as a result of our reasoning processes which at best "see through a glass darkly." After all, if God is who the Bible says he is, he must finally transcend our reasoning. Rather this assurance is a gift of God himself who by his Spirit ministers in our hearts bearing witness that "we are children of God" (Rom 8:16). For he must not only open our eyes to see what is true but also condition our hearts to obey what we have seen. Yet this witness comes not apart from our reasoning, but in and through it. Austin Farrer comments: "How through finite categories, there comes to be known an infinite being which distends and bursts them, may well seem a wonder; but it is so" (p. 54). All we need insist is that the One who is revealed must not overthrow the rational conditions in which we find ourselves, but rather confirm them. And this is just what we find to be the case with the God of the Bible.

Questions for Review
1. What lines of reasoning establish the truth of Christianity?
2. How does F. R. Tennant argue for the existence of God?
3. What is one weakness in Tennant's argument for Christianity?
4. Explain J. W. Montgomery's argument from history.
5. What are two weaknesses of Montgomery's approach?
6. How does Cornelius Van Til argue for Christianity, and how does his way differ from Montgomery's?
7. How does E. J. Carnell broaden Van Til's method?
8. How does Francis Schaeffer use cultural apologetics?
9. How can Christian experience argue for Christian truth?
10. What are "redemptive analogies"?
11. How does John Hick describe faith?
12. What does Basil Mitchell mean by a "cumulative case"?

CHAPTER FOUR

Basic Framework: Christianity as the Project of God

I n the last chapter we saw that arguments for Christianity must include three elements: empirical, logical and personal. Empirical factors are fundamental. Christianity rests on specific events in the life of Israel and of Christ which are subject to historical examination. We must also employ rational methods as we seek to understand God and the world as a coherent whole. But since human life is characterized by mystery and wonder, it cannot be fully comprehended by empirical description or logical formulae. Furthermore, we seek not so much absolute proof as removal of ignorance and insight into truth; we must therefore use personal as well as historical and rational arguments. As John Hick points out, we do not so much infer God from our experience as become conscious of living in his presence. This consciousness becomes as compelling as our consciousness of the natural world (1966, p. 210); it moreover demands active personal response and not only intellectual assent. All of this suggests that we need a comprehensive model of Christianity that will include all three ways of understanding the faith and commending it to others. It is the purpose of this chapter to construct such a model.

It is strange that Christianity should be accused of irrelevance. Paul would surely have been puzzled by such a charge. He says boldly in Romans 1:16: "I am not ashamed of the gospel: it is the power of God for salvation to every one who has faith." If we do not see the gospel as *power*, we may suspect something is wrong with our understanding of it.

What is to blame for the supposed irrelevance of the gospel? I believe the fault lies within the basic framework in which we present it. All too often we think of Christianity as only a *system of thought* that we must defend and convince people of. The faith once for all committed to the saints becomes a body of truths that we can put before people in the form of a creed, confession or statement of faith. It would be foolish to deny the importance of such expressions of faith; indeed scholars have found such statements in the New Testament itself (1 Timothy 3:16 may be an example). But if we limit our model of Christianity to these expressions, we may seriously limit the power of the gospel to function in our everyday lives.

Reasons for such limitation are not hard to find. Since the Enlightenment in the West, educated people have spent an inordinate amount of time discussing how it is that we can know anything. As a result philosophy has recently been far more concerned with epistemology (the study of knowledge) than with either metaphysics or axiology (questions of being or value). Ironically we have believed this has brought about a progressive "enlightenment" of our understanding, which in practice means that we understand life less and less as having any relationship to God. Since we know how things happen "scientifically," we have no need to bring God into the picture to account for them. This process of secularization has made God seem more and more remote from people's lives. Is Christianity indeed the power of God?

To answer this question I would like to propose an apologetic model: Christianity is a *project of God*. That is, Christianity tells what God has done, is doing and will do in the world, and what we must do in response to his actions. An illustration may make this model clear. Suppose we discover that a time bomb set to go off in fifteen minutes has been placed beneath the floor of our home. We might respond by sitting and discussing the properties of bombs, the force of explosions and the meanness of people who plant bombs; but the more intelligent response would be to leave the house as quickly as possible. Likewise, though there is much to understand about Christianity, if the gospel is the power of God there is also something to be done.

In the literature of missiology, Alan Tippett has used the term *power encounter* to describe the confrontation of Christianity with other religious systems. According to Scripture, humanity exists in a conflict of the powers, in the struggle of Satan against God. People are forced to act and decide; they must take sides in this great struggle, and the Spirit of the biblical God must be shown to be greater, more powerful than rival spirits and gods (1969, pp. 88-89). This is an actual power confrontation taking place in people's experience, not merely a theoretical conflict which must be understood. When Christianity arrived in the Solomon Islands, Tippett notes,

> the religious encounter was not between a pagan deity and a Christian God. The encounter had to take place on the level of daily life against those powers which dealt with the relevant problems of gardening, fishing, war, security, food supply and personal life crises. For all these mana (power) was needed. In the eyes of any potential Melanesian convert to Christianity, there, the issue was one of *power in daily life*. (1967, p. 5)

Conversions resulted from the confrontation of the power of God with Melanesian animist deities (1967, pp. 44, 101). On the other hand, as D. J. Gelpi points out, in communities where the power of the Spirit is not evident, grace will probably not be experienced or be evident to outsiders (p. 108). If the One indwelling Christian communities is greater than the powers of the world, then a power confrontation ought to be a powerful demonstration of the gospel reality (1 Jn 4:4). And while many Westerners have ceased to believe in the spiritual dimensions of the human condition, most non-Western peoples accept without question the influence of spirits and powers. Whether these are real evil spirits or merely community laws and taboos, they actually bind people and speak of the need for the liberating power of the gospel.

Someone might ask if such an approach is legitimate in apologetics, ordinarily thought to defend the truth of Christian belief. Could not false faith successfully confront powers that bind people? But truth, as we noted earlier, must be more broadly understood. As Luther put it, only that God is true who is Creator of heaven and earth. Truth says not only that certain facts are true or have happened, but, more important, "this is how things are for me." Scripture does not hesitate to present God's reality in terms of a power confrontation, whether on Mt. Carmel or Golgotha. Although of course such events must be considered rationally and defended historically, they constitute the stuff of biblical revelation. Looking at Christianity as a project of God must include these other factors as well. But for many people questions of power and reality may be the determining factor in coming to belief. For the truth that makes men and women free is that which provides both insight into the way things are and power to make things new.

Let us then examine this picture of Christianity to see if it holds true. We will approach the matter from three directions: biblical, historical and personal.

Biblical Basis

The Bible pictures God as an active, personal presence in history. Though existing eternally in communion with himself, God spoke the world into being to embody and reflect his glory (Ps 33:6), and he continues to uphold it with his sustaining presence

(Ps 104). Adam and Eve, however, fled from the loving presence of God and declared their independence from his purposes (Gen 3). The rest of the biblical record can be read as God's sovereign search and rescue of the fallen creation. Biblical students call this great search the kingdom of God. Read in this light, history is the account of God's intervention in the created order to restore fellowship and communion with his creation. The biblical account revolves around certain pivotal events wherein God acts to restore the fallen order. These events include the exodus wherein God delivered his people from bondage in Egypt and became their salvation (Ex 15:1-19), and his guidance of Israel into the land of promise where he "planted" them (v. 17; Ps 80:8). Later, though they had been driven out because of their sin, God gathered them again to their homeland. These great gestures of God which provide the backbone of history (and orient our own histories) come to a mighty climax in the work of Christ. Here God's delivering power comes to the concrete manifestation of the kingdom of God (Mt 12:28). Christ, through his life, death and resurrection, has triumphed over the powers of evil (Col 2:15). At Pentecost God poured out his Spirit upon his people and equipped them to be his emissaries (Eph 4:8-12).

The Bible pictures history as the arena in which God is working out his purposes, as a lump of dough being permeated by the leaven of the kingdom of God (Mt 13:33). God's kingdom will grow until the mountain of the Lord is established as the highest of the mountains (Is 2:2). As the progress of history is marked by the strong hand of God, so the Bible presents the end of history as a mighty intervention to bring judgment and final deliverance. That last day will be a fearful and wonderful unveiling of power, the explosion of the time bomb which the Bible tells us is ticking in the created order.

These events and their inspired elaboration in Scripture provide a framework for understanding the world and its history: God's eternal power is working to accomplish his project of reconciling the world to himself. If an event is to be understood, the Christian claims, it must be seen in its place in God's project.

When biblical stories are seen this way, we believe, they display a coherence that supports the Christian view of God's character.

Historical Support

If the Christian faith is anchored in history, we should be able to find public evidences of its power. The Christian claims that such support is not lacking. Within secular history God's kingdom activity is clearly visible to those with eyes to see it. The primary evidence exists in the worldwide spread and vitality of the Christian church. From a small, embattled sect of Judaism, Christianity has grown into the only religion with substantial presence virtually throughout the world. W. H. C. Frend concludes his study of the early church by noting that, before A. D. 300, chances of suppressing Christianity had diminished: "The Church had become a great popular movement" (p. 571). The movement has continued to gather momentum up to our day. Church historian Kenneth Scott Latourette concludes his monumental five-volume work on the spread of Christianity with these words:

> The continued geographic spread of Christianity and its continued rootage in other peoples than Europeans in an age when forces issuing from the perversion of the faith in the former Christendom have been mounting are evidence of vigour and universality. The ecclesiastical bodies through which the faith has spread have never been pure embodiments of the faith. In them, as in individual Christians, have existed contradictions between aspiration and attainment. Yet in them the fruits of the Spirit have been present. (pp. 533-34)

Let us note some evidence for this powerful presence of Christianity.

No religion has had the effect of Christianity on *linguistics*. Wherever Christianity has gone, it has concerned itself with language and translation. Believing in the importance of the revealed Word of God, Christians have worked to make it as widely available as possible. Ulfilas, the apostle to the Goths (ca 311-83), invented a special alphabet for the Gothic language and translated the Bible into it. Christian respect for language and writing, in fact, may lie at the heart of today's understanding of literature that we take for granted. Certainly William Carey's zeal to collect Hindu literature, growing out of his Christian convictions, greatly influenced other early Hindu collections. The formative role of Luther's Bible on the German language, the King James Bible on English, and Calvin's Institutes on French is undisputed. Today the work of Christian translators like the Summer Institute of Linguistics has contributed to the preservation of many indigenous traditions.

It is hard to overemphasize this valuing of language and written traditions, especially since Christianity is often accused of destroying ancient customs. F. S. Downs notes the role Christianity played in the modernization of northeast India:

> Christianity contributed to this process, but it would have happened anyway; what Christianity did was to provide the people with an ideology and the tools (literature, etc.) to make the changes without losing their sense of identity. It also ensured that they would retain control of their own institutions. (p. 26)

The Christian respect for Indian written tradition typifies the church's influence in many other parts of the world.

Christianity has also fostered *education* wherever its missionaries have gone. Believing in the necessity of enscripturated revelation and in man's dignity as God's image bearer, Christians have always been concerned to teach their converts to read and write. The European monastery and cathedral schools of the Middle Ages are the foundation of the whole Western educational system. In parts of the Third World, the most outstanding educational institutions were started by missionaries; one often hears of African leaders who had their basic education in mission schools.

Christian missionaries have provided *medicine* and *hospitals* throughout the world. Ida Scudder, daughter of a missionary to India, was appalled at the way Hindu women died in childbirth because they would not be treated by male doctors. At a time when female physicians were rare, she trained in medicine and returned to India to work. Her dedication resulted in a superb hospital and school, with a motor clinic reaching out into the countryside, to treat Hindu women and to train doctors and nurses.

Then Christianity has championed *women's rights*. William Carey fought for years against the Indian practice of *suttee* (burning widows on their husbands' funeral pyres) and finally succeeded in obtaining a decree against it. Missionaries fought also to abolish the Chinese practice of footbinding.

All these reforms grew out of the Christian view that all people are God's creation and stand equally before him, a view emphasized by the independent church movement following the Reformation. Hendrik Kraemer has said this movement's stress on individual responsibility before God led to our modern idea of *democracy*. "In these circles the creative seeds and patterns of what is now called democratic way of life have not only been born, but have yielded the prefiguration" (p. 26).

The gospel has also stimulated various *social reforms*. In the eighteenth and nineteenth centuries, English movements for basic education, limited working hours, better housing, child labor laws and the freeing of slaves were sponsored by Christians. Earle Cairns comments: "This social transformation was due to an enlightened social conscience, alert statesmen of principle and humane colonial legislators. These statesmen and legislators accepted their responsibilities as citizens because they had become Christians. This enlightened social conscience was mainly the result of rival after 1739" (p. 56). In America there are clearly Christian roots to movements for equal treatment of women and for racial reform.

Of course Christians have not always lived up to the principles of the gospel. Moreover they have often suffered for their faith. Nevertheless one can argue from Scripture that the goal of God's historical program is to overcome evil. The resurrection proclaims that God has triumphed and will one day make his rule known, even though the Bible warns that every advance of the kingdom will be contested by the powers of evil until a final apostasy and the antichrist appear. But Scriptures indicate that all these challenges are "part of the process of the growth of Christ's rule and not a peculiar terminal exception to it" (Lovelace, p. 416). Meanwhile Christians are called upon to model themselves after Christ who came not to be ministered unto but to minister. This life of ministry often leads to suffering and sometimes to death. But such suffering, Paul says, is not worthy to be compared with the glory that will be revealed in God's children (Rom 8:18).

God is at work in history, and we often see signs of his presence. His kingdom, however, sometimes appears in the form of weakness rather than strength. His action is sometimes hidden in suffering and failure. But this too, as Lesslie Newbigin points out, is consistent with the meaning of Christianity. "The presence of the Kingdom, hidden and revealed in the cross of Jesus, is carried through history hidden and revealed in the life of the community which bears in its life the dying and rising of Jesus" (p. 58). Though the dark side of history must not be overlooked, Christians are not defeatists. They expect God's intervention and have already tasted the heavenly kingdom.

The obvious contributions of Christianity are only the tip of the iceberg. The real miracles are less visible but more widespread: the work of forgiveness and renewal that God does in hearts, families and communities in countless unknown places and unremembered times. Renewal is possible because Christians believe God has started something in history that he will carry to conclusion, a mighty climax that will settle all debts and right all injustices.

Personal Potential

Our model of Christianity as the project of God makes it easy to return to the theme of personal relevance. If history reflects God's project of restoration, if its direction and goals are determined by his purposes and the end that is approaching, then the human family stands in a position of accountability. Men and women must come to terms with God's program; they must accept his lordship and work to further his purposes, or they will destroy themselves by their rebellion. The last days, as the New Testament tells us, require decision. Time moves inexorably toward its own end, and we stand in the room where the time bomb is ticking. If history is a great drama, we are actors not spectators. We must therefore respond to the movement of the play and speak our parts.

History is not a series of remote events which do not concern us, but a movement in which we are vitally involved. Our eternal destiny is determined by our response to that movement. Life is not an endless round of activities, work and concern. It is a pilgrimage with a definite goal, an end toward which we are moving. And behind and within all the events of the journey we meet a personal God who seeks our fellowship and service.

For the Christian, life offers the challenge of furthering God's project. On the one hand this means that the loving presence of God will be visible in communities that come together in his name. Openness, forgiveness and hospitality will characterize such fellowships. On the other hand Christians may join God's renewal program in the world. This means Christians may dare to form concrete (rather than intellectual) hypotheses about the world; they must make plans and not only have opinions. If it is true that Christianity is a project in history by which God is doing something about the world's fallen condition, then it is also true that we can work with him toward this end. We are reminded of the words of Miguez-Bonino:

> The gospel invites and drives us to make concrete historical options and assures them eschatological permanence insofar as they represent the qualities of human exietence which correspond to the Kingdom. We can, therefore, within human history, engage with other men in action which is significant in terms of God's redemptive purpose, of his announced and promised future kingdom. (1975, p. 150)

Our work may reflect God's kingdom—this may seem only a dream. But remember Peter's promise at Pentecost: by the Spirit would come renewed ability to "dream dreams" and "see visions" of what God can do (Acts 2:17 quoting Joel 2:28-32). For as Christ has given us "power to become children of God" (Jn 1:12), so he can make God's kingdom visible not "in talk but in power" (1 Cor 4:20), the very power of him who "delivered us from the dominion of darkness and transferred us to the kingdom of his beloved Son" (Col 1:13). Clearly if this power is not seen in our lives and in our communities, it is more a reproach to our faith than an argument against Christianity.

The rational analysis of ideas is important to our faith, but Christianity is far more than a system of thought. The movement that we yearn for and that Scriptures promise is not of ideas but of events, of days hastening on to a climax, of a mighty popular movement. Christianity is the powerful project of God. We are bidden to join it, and we may give it our all.

Questions for Review
1. What is the source of the tendency to consider Christianity a system of ideas?
2. Explain what Alan Tippett means by a power confrontation.
3. What is the significance of redemptive events in Scripture?
4. How has Christianity influenced linguistics? Education? Human Rights?
5. How can you reflect God's project in your community?

PART TWO

Meeting Specific Challenges to Christianity

CHAPTER FIVE

Alternative Frameworks to Christianity

N ow that we have suggested a framework that expresses the Christian faith, we are ready to examine specific challenges that Christians face today. Christianity does not stand alone in having to defend itself against objections raised by unbelievers. Every religious or philosophical commitment must be able to defend itself from attack and commend itself to those outside its ranks. Yet Christians often feel threatened when faced with articulate unbelievers. So many powerful alternatives to the Christian view seem to exist today.

In fact, however, there are really few general frameworks from which to choose. We can categorize them in three groups. The first group includes theists who believe in a personal God who has created the world and who, though separate from his creation, is working in it to achieve his purposes. This is the view we have advanced in the preceding chapters. In the second group are those who deny the existence of any god and claim that the natural world and its processes are all that exist. These people are called naturalists or materialists. Third, some deny that anything is natural and insist that God (or an absolute spirit or spirits) pervades and controls all that exists. Thus spiritual purpose is present in all reality, and if you insist on seeing anything in a natural way, you are not being true to the nature of reality. These people are called idealists or sometimes pantheists (if they say God is identical with everything that exists).

Clearly, a religious (or philosophical) commitment is not optional: it is a necessity for living a truly human life and for making intelligent value judgments. The question is not *whether* you will commit yourself to something, but *to what*. Will this commitment stand up under scrutiny? Let's examine naturalism and idealism, the two alternatives to theism, to see if they offer the strong challenge to Christianity that is sometimes claimed.

Naturalism

A common view among educated people is called *naturalism*. Naturalism is often associated with *materialism,* the view that matter is the ultimate reality, but it is logically distinct from it. Naturalism is more a method of dealing with reality than a belief about its nature. It is not surprising that the West, where this view is prominent, is good at developing methods and techniques but not always good at setting ultimate goals reflecting the nature of reality. Here is a definition of naturalism by one of its adherents:

A philosophical position, empirical in method, that regards everything that exists or occurs to be conditioned in its existence or occurrence by causal factors within one all-encompassing system of nature, however "spiritual" or purposeful or rational some of these things and events may in their functions and values prove to be. (S. P. Lamprecht in Krikorian, p. 18)

The key word in this system is *natural.* The whole universe is made up of natural objects, that is, things that have come into existence by natural causes. No entities or events can lie outside this natural causal system and thus beyond the scope of scientific explanation. Whatever the nature or function of a natural object, it must have as its cause another object or a part of the history of an object (such as disintegration, germination or photosynthesis). As far as our knowledge of the world is concerned, only the operation of natural processes is explanatory. Therefore reference to non-natural objects (God or spirits) cannot be explanatory.

It might be objected that we cannot explain everything that exists. But the naturalist would respond that his or her commitment is to the principle that the natural order is made up of all natural processes and that everything is thus in principle naturally explainable (even if there are parts of the process that we cannot yet explain). Naturalists recognize that this is a faith commitment, but they believe that apart from such a commitment, it is not possible to know anything at all. The common person often uses this natural method for finding out about the world; the scientist simply uses a more sophisticated version of this method in the laboratory. Both assume that nature is ordered and that they can discover and make use of its laws. Humans ordinarily seek a natural explanation for things before turning to the supernatural; even in politics and morals we seek laws that can govern human behavior. Life cannot be lived in an orderly way unless reason is allowed to control our acts. What is true of the individual, says the naturalist, is true of society and the world at large.

The advantage of their view of things, according to naturalists, is that it is self-corrective. That is, if we discover by reflection and examination that a belief is incorrect, we can change it. Refusing to make an ultimate judgment about reality (a view called agnosticism) is not a defect. In fact such a refusal is really the only way to be "open" to the facts as we come to understand them.

This point of view is ancient. In the first century before Christ, the Roman philosopher Lucretius wrote a philosophical poem called *De rerum natura*. If we go by the evidence of our senses, he claimed, all we can say is that matter exists (the absence of matter is simply space). Any metaphysical speculation beyond this must be dismissed as too complicated. Everything can be explained, he believed, by the constant fall of atoms through a bottomless space. By an inexplicable swerve they join themselves together in different combinations to form all things that exist. This process adequately accounts for all that exists; there is no need for God or teleology (a doctrine of purpose). Simply in contemplating the order of the universe, Lucretius maintained, one can find joy and free himself from pain and worry.

In our own century the naturalist viewpoint has had a large following, especially in the West and by those trained in the scientific disciplines. The biologist Julian Huxley and the mathematician Bertrand Russell are two famous adherents of naturalism.

Julian Huxley, born to a family of famous scientists, made a mark for himself in biology. In 1929 he wrote *Religion without Revelation,* where he held that complete skepticism is impossible but that belief must be founded on proper evidence. He believed the hypothesis of God inadequate, in that "any set of phenomena can be treated by the method of science" (p. 13). Following the scientific method we find nothing "beyond" this world and conclude that the idea of God "has been put there by man" (p. 18). Giving up this belief is no great loss; in fact one experiences, Huxley claimed, a great sense of relief (pp. 32-33). The source of the erroneous belief in God, Huxley said, is the sense of the sacred lying at the basis of all religion. People personify this feeling as God. Such vague and uncertain feelings must be given up, and in their place we must formulate a belief system based on scientific truth. This substitute religion must be based entirely on verifiable evidence. It will issue in a common way of life based on chosen values and practices.

Huxley was committed to an evolutionary humanism. He believed: "Man's most sacred duty and at the same time his most glorious opportunity, is to promote the maximum fulfilment of the evolutionary process on this earth; and this includes the fullest realization of his own inherent possibilities" (p. 194). So while he gave up faith in God, Huxley retained faith in human possibilities. Pursuing a better world through understanding natural phenomena became his ultimate commitment.

Another famous naturalist is Bertrand Russell, who gave his testimony in the provocatively titled book, *Why I Am Not a Christian*. Russell believed that two fatal objections could be brought against religious belief. First, it seemed to him impossible to reconcile the presence of suffering and evil in the world with the existence of God. The happiness and well-being of humanity look unimportant in a view of the universe as a whole. Russell admitted that the existence of God cannot be disproved, but he believed that without verifiable evidence for his existence, one could just as well account for the world by spontaneous creation. This may seem odd, but, he insisted, no law of nature rules out odd occurrences.

Russell's second major objection to religious belief is its supposed harmfulness. Believing something unprovable forces you to close your mind to any further evidence that might count against your faith. Far better to support your views with reason and to be open to the evidence wherever it may lead. Religious belief, furthermore, leads to structures that repress dissent and stifle the free investigation of science. Russell considered only the harmful effects of faith; any beneficial effects passed unnoticed. His treatment of Christ shows a similar inconsistency. In Russell's judgment, Christ's defective teachings (such as those on hell and judgment) far outweigh his positive contribution. Russell concluded: "Either in the matter of virtue or in the matter of wisdom, Christ does not stand as high as some other people known to history" (p. 19), specifically Socrates and Buddha.

Russell admitted that his view of a godless world is gloomy. On his ninety-second birthday he said, "The secret of happiness is to face the fact that the world is horrible." The only order that exists is that imposed by the human mind, and even this is ephemeral and transitory. Yet Russell's framework was not only the result of impartial scientific investigation. It was also an existential faith commitment:

That man is the product of causes which had no prevision of the end they were achieving; that his origin, his growth, his

hopes and fears, his loves and his beliefs, are but the outcome
of accidental collocations of atoms; . . . that all the labours of
the ages, all the devotion, all the aspirations, all the noonday
brightness of human genius, are destined to extinction in the
vast death of the solar system . . .—all these things, if not quite
beyond dispute, are yet so nearly certain, that no philosophy
which rejects them can hope to stand. Only within the scaffold-
ing of these truths, only on the firm foundation of unyielding
despair, can the soul's habitation henceforth be safely built.
(Quoted in Burtt, p. 23)
What kind of response can a Christian make to this viewpoint?
Let us first deal with the charge that Christians are closed-minded
while scientific naturalists can be open to the truth wherever it
may be found. This is a serious charge, for it implies that Christians are not sincere in their pursuit of truth. But are naturalists
necessarily more open-minded than people with a religious faith?
This may be doubted. For naturalists not only insist that truth be
supported by empirical evidence; they also claim that no truth lies
beyond the scope of scientific explanation, and that if any transcendent truth did exist we could never know about it. But to
make such statements is to close one's mind to the possibility that
truth may be discovered by other than scientific means; that it
might, say, be revealed by God. One wonders whether such a
limitation on knowledge can be supported by empirical evidence.
Now it may or may not be true that truth can be known by mystical experience or by revelation, but such claims deserve to be
examined. The scientific method of knowing truth must not be
allowed to declare all other methods invalid. As Russell himself
insisted, order and unity are merely human inventions which
form themselves into various paradigms by which we know the
world. Thus, even on Russell's own terms it is hard to see how
the scientific method provides definitive knowledge and why it
alone must be allowed to take the field.

But let us grant for a moment that we must have evidence if
we are to believe in the supernatural. Does the scientific method
completely exclude the possibility of such evidence? Science is

based on the premise that the world is intelligible. Does not the idea of intelligibility raise metaphysical or transcendent questions that naturalism cannot easily answer? Why and how is the world intelligible? The Christian attributes intelligibility to God's creative design; Russell insists that the world is intelligible spontaneously. While Lord Russell is entitled to his opinion, he may not claim a privileged position for the concept of spontaneity; this is not intrinsically more probable than the theistic explanation.

The Christian can press his case further. If naturalists are open to the facts, then they must be open to the possibility that not all facts are available or amenable to scientific methods. Religious facts may be persuasive even without being scientifically verifiable. For example, Christians claim a common personal experience of Christ that sustains them in their daily lives. Such a claim is at least prima facie evidence for the truth of the experience. If the experience is delusive, the burden of proof is on those accounting for it in other ways.

And what of the good effects of religion? May these not count as evidence for the truth of the Christian claim? Moreover a very important source of evidence lies in the future, obviously outside the area of scientific proof: the return of Christ and the new heaven and new earth. What now seems meaningless and unjust, from our limited point of view, may turn out to make sense when all the evidence is in. It is true that the Christian walks by faith and not by sight, but everyone's final commitment—not only the Christian's—goes beyond the evidence at hand.

As we will argue in a later chapter, Christians do not seek to invalidate the findings of science. The question is rather whether a final commitment to the naturalist world view is justified in light of all the evidence—empirical, logical and personal. The confrontation should not be between science and Christianity but between a world view shaped by scientific methodology and one shaped by the Christian framework. Christians insist that knowing God provides a richer and fuller view of life than the naturalist hypothesis allows, for the Christian view features the human values the naturalist treasures and provides a larger context in which these values have meaning. Perhaps the world is richer in significance than the naturalist is ready to admit. Even if some of the evidence is ambiguous and can be interpreted differently by the Christian and by the naturalist, both positions cannot be true. We must decide to make a faith commitment and live our lives in the light of our decision.

Idealism

Eastern religious philosophy. If naturalism is the characteristic world view in Western countries, idealism characterizes much of Eastern thought. Though there have been idealist philosophers in the West, we will consider that stream of idealism expressed in Indian philosophy, especially in the Upanishads (800-500 B. C.) and the Bhagavad-Gita (ca 300-200 B. C.). Although we will limit our discussion to that period of Indian philosophy, idealism has been influential throughout Asia, not only in the various schools of Hinduism but also in Buddhism and Jainism. Eastern philosophy presents the interpreter with a bewildering variety of religious ideas, and we do not claim that what we will say covers all forms of it. But we will try to present basic and characteristic ideas.

We have seen that naturalism characteristically takes a scientific attitude: it applies scientific and logical categories to the world order. Idealism, on the other hand, takes primarily a religious attitude: reflection on the world is not to understand and master reality but rather to achieve salvation, or release, through mystical experience. Because of these differing attitudes, the language of Eastern religion, even when using words also used in the West, usually has a widely different meaning from the language of Western philosophy. Since the goal of Eastern philosophy is an experience of reality rather than a careful understanding of it, the language used is often imprecise and, from a Western point of view, ambiguous. This may not be a fault if the goal is contemplation rather than comprehension. I have had Asian friends ask me, "Why do you Westerners always have to understand? Can you not appreciate and contemplate the mystery you see?" But this approach, in spite of its values, does make comparison of Eastern and Western ideas difficult. As one interpreter has said, nothing can be said of Hinduism that cannot also be denied.

It follows that idealism's challenge to Christianity is less direct and therefore more insidious than the challenge offered by naturalism. Whereas naturalism has been formed partly under Christian influence, idealism belongs to an entirely different universe of discourse. And while idealism may employ some familiar expressions—indeed some of them have a biblical ring—Eastern religion's orientation toward the world is incompatible at essential points with Christianity's.

Eastern philosophy's basic assumption is that all reality belongs to a continuum; all reality is ultimately one. Although this view, called *monism*, has been variously interpreted, it gives Eastern religion its characteristic flavor. There is one single indestructible reality—the *Brahman*—in which all things participate; thus the most humble element of reality shares its essence with the most exalted. The goal is not to understand this—interpretations are often widely contradictory—so much as to experience it and to direct one's life in its light. Reverence for the cow, for example, shows insight into the unity of all reality. Let us discuss four key concepts of this world view and see what challenge they offer to a Christian world view.

In the East one begins with the *Atman*, or the self, because this is the reality that is immediately experienced. This should not be confused with Western empirical concepts such as the soul or the personality, notions that have been abstractly elaborated and can be conceptually known. The ideal of knowledge in the East is not the subject-object knowledge that we prize in the West. To the Eastern philosopher, objective knowledge is a lesser mode that ideally gives way to immediate or intuitive knowledge. We begin with the Atman, therefore, because self-knowledge is immediate. It is the highest form of knowledge we can have; I cannot know another person as I know myself.

Our desires and emotions may produce the impression that we are isolated and individual, but this comes from ignorance and is not the primary experience of the self. When we lose this false sense of individuality we see that our pure consciousness expresses the unity of self with all reality. This awareness brings us to the second major idea, that of Brahman, or the One. The supreme achievement of the Upanishads is its insistence that to experience Atman is to know Brahman:

> Now, that which is the subtle essence—in it all that exists has its self. That is the True. That is the Self. That thou art. (Chhandogya Upanishad VI, xii, 3)

This understanding comes by immediate insight; we understand when our eyes are opened:

> This soul of mine within the heart is smaller than a grain of rice or a barley-corn, or a mustard-seed, or a grain of millet, or the kernel of a grain of millet; this soul of mine within the heart is greater than the earth, greater than the atmosphere, greater than the sky, greater than the worlds. . . . This soul of mine within the heart, this is Brahman. (Chhand III, xiv, 3)

If we remember that the self and the nonself, Atman and Brahman, are basically one, we are not deluded or led astray. Atman in one sense is the Brahman subjectively considered; Brahman is Atman from an objective point of view, or, as Bouquet put it, the "verbal image of the sacred or holy" (p. 129). But of course we cannot know Brahman apart from our knowledge of the self.

Exactly how Brahman is to be described, and how much reality the individual self is to have, is much debated in Hindu (and Buddhist) traditions; different answers have given rise to different schools. But basically the Brahman is described in two ways. The first way, called the all-cosmic, emphasizes that the One is full of good qualities and refers to "him" in almost personal categories. Perhaps this Brahman is identified with the individual and thus described in expressions related to human experience. The second way, called the acosmic (which became the characteristic method of Buddhism), believes the One is without qualities, indeterminate; it is the impersonal absolute which can be described only in a negative way. From this point of view the world and the self are unreal, mere appearance.

Insight into the unity of Atman and Brahman is the ideal toward which people must strive. Ordinarily we are misled by our experience. This leads us to the third major conception in Eastern religion: *maya*, or illusion. This term was not formally articulated until much later in Hindu philosophy, but the idea is clearly present in the Upanishads and the Gita. Because the One appears in an infinite number of forms or effects, we are sometimes distracted by this pulsating appearance. We find the form so dazzling that we take our mind off the inner contents. Much like Plato in the West, Eastern teachers explained that we are deluded by this world of shadow and crookedness. As Krishna (the form that the One takes in the Gita) explains to his disciple Arjuna: "My mysterious cloud of appearance is hard to pass beyond; but those who in truth come to me go beyond the world of shadows" (7.14). Attachment to the world is most often called "desire." When we desire some object we imply separateness between the self and the desired object. We are thus distracted from experiencing the unity of all reality and enchained by appearance.

The fourth major concept of Eastern religion is therefore the goal of true philosophy: *moksha,* or release. This final experience, which Buddhism later called nirvana, is the immediate insight into reality, the state of final bliss. We must be careful to understand this correctly. Though we are using terms having to do with knowledge, this is not knowledge of or about something but rather an experience of nonduality. A verse from the Manukya Upanishad expresses this clearly: "Turiya [the state of highest blessedness] is not that which is conscious of the inner world . . . nor the outer world . . . nor both. It is not simple consciousness nor is It unconsciousness. It is unperceived, unrelated, incomprehensible, uninferable, unthinkable, and undescribable. . . . It is the cessation of all phenomena; It is all peace, all bliss, non-dual" (Mand. 7).

To explain moksha, reference is often made to levels of human consciousness. Ordinarily when we are awake we are aware of the external world and distracted by its character. When we are asleep we experience only the self; yet, though this is a type of the highest bliss, there is something still higher, because sleep often makes us aware of the world through dreams. The higher state is a waking trance in which the self is disciplined to such an extent that the world is not experienced and awareness of the One is complete. This experience makes it possible for Hindu saints to walk through fire without being burned, to sleep on painful nails and to perform other superhuman feats. But even this experience is a type of something still higher, when a person is released from the cycle of birth and rebirth and has immediate awareness of bliss.

A person may strive after this final experience by means of rigorous disciplines, or *yogas*. We will mention the three most important. The *jñana yoga*, or way of knowledge, is a severe mental discipline through which one achieves insight by reflection upon reality. One comes to be "firmly rooted in higher reason and [is] unmoved by the pair of opposites" (Gita 6.22). The person ceases to be moved by joy and sorrow because by knowledge (insight) he or she has transcended such distinctions.

The *karma yoga*, or way of action, is especially prominent in the Gita (from which the following references are taken). This expresses in another form the interrelationship of all reality. No action is without its consequence, and our actions in one life determine our state in a future existence. There are many kinds of action—sacrifice, good works, fighting in a noble war—but only one thing makes them virtuous: acting without seeking the fruit of action. The wise man acts "unselfishly for the good of all the world" (3.25). As Krishna explains: "There is no man on earth who can fully renounce living work, but he who renounces the reward of his work is in truth a man of renunciation" (18.11). No good is lost. Even if it is inadequate it will serve as the basis for building in some future life.

The *bhakti yoga,* or way of devotion to God (in the Gita to Krishna himself), uses words familiar to Christians: love, faith and even mercy. Krishna says:

> To those who are ever in harmony, and who worship me with their love, I give the Yoga of vision and with this they come to me. In my mercy I dwell in their hearts and I dispel their darkness of ignorance by the lamp of wisdom. (10.10-11)

And: "The greatest of all Yogis is he who with all his soul has faith and he who with all his soul loves me" (6:47). But it would be a mistake to understand these terms literally. Krishna may represent the Brahman in a personal form (see 10.12), but reality transcends the forms in which it appears and can never be identified with them:

All this visible universe comes from my invisible Being. All beings have their rest in me, but I have not my rest in them. And in truth they rest not in me: consider my sacred mystery. I am the source of all beings, I support them all, but I rest not in them. (9. 4, 5)

This conception gives rise to the Hindu belief in *avatar*, or the manifestation of God in human form. The One finds expression in certain holy men, one of whom, they are very willing to say, is Jesus Christ. We will presently note how different the avatar is from the Christian idea of Incarnation.

These yogas—and others we have not considered—provide ways to strive for salvation or release. Emphasis on various yogas has led to different schools and even traditions of Eastern thought (traditions that are not always compatible with one another). But in Atman, Brahman, maya, moksha and yoga, we see a sketch of the world view underlying Hindu religion.

Christian response to Eastern religion. Christians often first react to Eastern spirituality by appreciating its thoroughly spiritual interpretation of reality. The famous Indian Christian Sundar Singh, when traveling in the West, couldn't get over his horror at the crass materialism he saw even among so-called Christians. The Eastern view of reality, he thought, was in some ways closer to the biblical picture of God and the world. There are striking parallels between biblical statements and Hindu Scriptures— being in but not of the world, not being led astray by desires, knowing the spirit by means of the spirit, and so forth.

Hinduism as well as Christianity sees the person as a moral being responsible to the surrounding moral order. But beneath this surface similarity lies an unbridgeable gulf between God's self-revelation in the Bible and the teachings of the Indian mystics. We will first look at problems in Hinduism's general framework and then contrast Hindu and biblical teachings.

The most serious problems in Hinduism lie in its conceptions of God and the world. If knowledge of the world is characterized by illusion, it is hard to see how any standard can prove illusion false (Hackett, pp. 158-75). Nor is it possible to see how immediate awareness of the One can be distinguished from any other awareness, since it has by definition transcended all distinctions. Moreover, at least for some Hindus, even this highest truth is in the last analysis part of the maya or cosmic illusion. While immediate or intuitive experience is a dimension of knowledge (knowledge of people has this character to it), without empirical or rational control there seems to be no way to make various notions—such as the undifferentiated unity of being, for example—intelligible or to communicate them to others. In this respect Zen Buddhism is more consistent when it attempts simply to evoke such experiences of oneness rather than to describe or commend them in any systematic way. While claiming allegiance to universal moral order, the Hindu view of maya ultimately undermines the reality of such an order or, at least, the possibility of knowing anything about it. Let us see how Christianity provides a satisfactory alternative to Eastern views.

1. Brahman and God. The Eastern conception of God maintains that something transcends God's personal being, even though God can appear in personal form and may be said to have personal qualities. Personhood is finally only a part of the world of appearance. In spite of personal references in Eastern thought and even a form of theistic dualism that appeared later during the Middle Ages, in no sense is God personally free to intervene in the world order and bring about value. Because God can take no initiative, there can be no fixed reference point for measuring progress or value. Moreover it seems impossible to preserve transcendence and perfection in a God who is united with a changing world characterized by evil and corruption.

2. The world and creation. Because the visible order belongs to the realm of shadow and appearance, it is impossible in Eastern

thought for it to have any final value. Experience is finally an illusion. The Bible insists that God is the source and end of all that is, and that his presence pervades creation, upholds it and causes it to reflect his character; but rather than giving the world a shadowy or ephemeral character, his presence gives creation substance and value. The creation therefore is to be affirmed, enjoyed and developed as an end in itself and not only as a means to a higher end. God promises this order will pass away only because he intends to make out of it a new order more nearly reflecting his values. In fact, the permanence of God's new order guarantees the permanence of God's relation with his people: "For as the new heavens and the new earth which I will make shall remain before me, says the LORD, so shall your descendants and your name remain" (Is 66:22). For in the biblical view it is never the material character of the world that is its handicap or that must somehow be transcended, but rather the distortion caused by human disobedience. Meanwhile the natural order is a positive value, not because God is in it but because at creation he gave it its own structure and value.

3. Karma and incarnation. Because the world has no intrinsic value in Eastern thought, the law of karma must finally be transcended. It cannot be creative. Since people are punished in a future life *by* their sins, they cannot be punished *for* them. Redemption, forgiveness and genuine release are not possible if the law of cause and effect is irreversible. Creativity and initiative can only be used to make the best of one's station, which after all cannot be changed. Here the Christian doctrine of incarnation is unique. Christ claimed to be much more than an appearance or a revelation of God. He did not come to show us something about God. He came as God to do something about this fallen created order. Because God is personal and loving, and because the world is good and ordered (though fallen), God could intervene and change the created order and his relation to it. Newness and forgiveness have become permanent characteristics of this world and potentially the experience of every creature in it. To the Christian, then, these words of Krishna in the Gita are impossible:

In every age I come back
To deliver the holy,
To destroy the sins of the sinner,
To establish righteousness. (In Ross, p. 28)
Not in every age, responds the Christian—once and for all.

4. Moksha and salvation. Finally, the Christian view of salvation has nothing in common with the Eastern view of release. One involves personal communion with a loving God; the other, timeless superpersonal union. The Bible clearly claims that the personal experience of salvation can never be transcended or denied ("Who shall separate us from the love of Christ?" Rom 8:35-39). Communion with God is not only a metaphor. Eastern thought makes the mistake that Greek philosophy and perhaps all nonrevealed religion tend to make. That mistake is to see knowledge, even the nondual, final experience of bliss, as the sufficient condition of salvation. Knowledge of the good is not enough, Christianity claims, nor is contemplation of the good or striving after it: all three are impossible because of human sin. One must be taken in hand by the transcendent personal God and transformed into his likeness. Nothing less than this is salvation; nothing more than this is possible or even desirable. "We shall be like him, for we shall see him as he is" (1 Jn 3:2).

The contrast between Hindu and Christian views of human involvement in the world is likewise striking. The intense mental concentration that Eastern religions advise and their attempt to harness all human powers in the spiritual quest are admirable but do not contribute to constructive life in the world. Even Transcendental Meditation instructors admit that the effects of meditation fade when one resumes normal activities. But, alas, normal activities are necessary to true human existence. Within the Christian framework human activity—the scientist's laboratory, the artist's studio—can create value and meaning. Moreover the spiritual discipline Christianity encourages—communion with God and meditation on his Word—heightens rather than diminishes both personal awareness and responsible life in the world.

The distinction is clear between Christianity and Eastern re-ligions. One can hear and answer the call of the personal God: "Come to me, all who labor and are heavy laden, and I will give you rest . . . for my yoke is easy" (Mt 11:28, 30). Or one can start down a long path of mind-breaking discipline, a path on which nothing is sure and at the end of which lies only what Albert Schweitzer called "world and life negation." Wanting things both ways, people often dislike choices. But that a choice is absolutely essential we hope to show in the next chapter.

Questions for Review

1. Describe the three basic views of the nature of reality.
2. Explain the method of naturalism.
3. Why can't a naturalist believe in God?
4. What is man's most sacred duty, according to Julian Huxley?
5. What are the two objections Russell makes against Christian-ity?
6. Describe three responses that a Christian might make to a naturalist.
7. In Eastern religions what is the relation between Brahman and Atman?
8. Describe the idea of salvation in Hinduism.
9. What are the three yogas or disciplines?
10. Explain the idea of karma.
11. How does the Christian idea of the world differ from the East-ern idea?
12. How is the Christian idea of salvation unique?
13. Why is the idea of a personal God essential to the Christian system?

CHAPTER SIX

Is Christianity for All or Only a Few?

Many people—both Christians and non-Christians—are troubled by the exclusivism of Christianity. How can we claim that only through faith in Jesus Christ can people be saved and that all who do not believe in him are condemned to hell? This problem deserves our serious attention. It divides itself into two questions which we will handle separately. The first asks about those who have never heard the gospel: Might God eventually save some or all of these? This is the question of universalism, the view that all will one day be saved. The second asks about Christianity's exclusive claims for Christ: Are there not other ways to God? This is the question of syncretism, the combination of various forms of religious belief.

Universalism

Many people do not understand how God can be just if he condemns those who have never heard the gospel; it seems that they are being condemned without ever having had a chance to be saved. If the work of Christ, which the Bible says is perfect and complete, is adequate for the sins of the whole world, why doesn't God accept it for all? And how can a good God allow some people to suffer eternally? Does this not impugn his love?

These objections have been raised inside the Christian family as well as outside. Christians have formulated the problem in various ways. Some are reluctant to decide on the issue one way or the other. The idea of judgment is so difficult to accept, these insist, that we should hold open the possibility of God's withholding his wrath. Karl Barth late in his life refused either to accept or reject universalism. Barth cautioned against surrendering to panic without carefully considering verses like Colossians 1:20, which says that God has determined "to reconcile to himself all things." Could this, Barth wonders, have a good meaning? Is the idea of universalism really more threatening than the gloomy legalistic theologian in our midst? "This much is certain," he concludes, "that we have no theological right to set any sort of limits to the lovingkindness of God which has appeared in Jesus Christ" (p. 60). D. T. Niles, an Indian theologian influenced by Barth, puts the problem this way:

Will all men be reclaimed? That is not our side of the problem. There are those who insist that no genuine and urgent conviction about the mission of the church is possible unless one is able to say positively: some will be saved and others will be damned. It is certainly true that those who are able to state the matter in this way do have a sense of urgency about their evangelistic and missionary responsibility; but the issue must nevertheless be pressed as to whether the whole drift of the New Testament allows for so simple and simplified a conviction. Can it be that anyone will reject him even at the last? . . . The New Testament does not lend itself to such speculation. It does not allow us to say either yes or no to the question "will all

men be saved?" *(Upon the Earth)*
Others, some of evangelical persuasion, insist that although God
will condemn those who reject him, some may believe on him
even without hearing the gospel. A. H. Strong writes:

> Since Christ is the Word of God and the Truth of God, he may
> be received even by those who have not heard of his manifesta-
> tion in the flesh. A proud and self-righteous morality is incon-
> sistent with saving faith; but a humble and penitent reliance
> upon God, as a Savior from sin and a guide of conduct, is an
> implicit faith in Christ; for such reliance casts itself upon God,
> so far as God has revealed himself,—and the only Revealer of
> God in Christ. We have, therefore, the hope that even among
> the heathen there may be some, like Socrates, who under the
> guidance of the Holy Spirit working through the truth of na-
> ture and conscience, have found the way to life and salvation.
> (p. 843)

He recounts missionary experiences where faith seems present
even before the gospel is preached, and notes that Scripture may
indicate this possibility in verses such as Matthew 8:11-12, pointing out nevertheless that such cases are rare. Salvation is not given
to those who "live up to the light they have" but rather to those
who, failing to live righteously, throw themselves upon the
mercy of God.

Still others totally repudiate the idea that God could condemn
any of his creation to eternal separation from him. Paul Tillich,
without minimizing the threat of "losing one's life," understands
this in terms of human finitude. In spite of the permanence of
existence, a person should hold open the possibility of wasting his
or her potentialities. The idea of a final division in which God
assigns people to heaven and hell, Tillich believes, is demonic, for
it introduces a split into the being of God himself since God is
the ground of all human existence. Says Tillich:

> From the point of view of the divine self-manifestation the doc-
> trine of twofold eternal destiny contradicts the idea of God's
> permanent creation of the finite as something "very good"
> (Genesis, chapter 1). If being as being is good . . . nothing that

is can become completely evil. If something is, if it has being, it is included in the creative divine love. (pp. 407-8)

While not all who reject the idea of eternal hell would accept Tillich's metaphysical framework, they would find his emphasis on God's love and the goodness of creation compelling.

How should we respond to these misgivings about eternal judgment? Let us divide our discussion into three sections: first, what man does; second, what God has done; and third, what is at stake.

To consider what people are doing about God is to appeal to empirical data: facts that may be observed by all and that figure prominently in the biblical record. It is clearly engraved on the human heart to seek after God or to make some ultimate commitment. People have an innate sense of God, and when this sense is repressed or ignored, as Psalm 14:1 implies, they make for themselves some God substitute. People respond to their sense of God or ultimate reality by seeking to order their lives accordingly. But experience and Scripture testify that we all fail to live up even to our own standards and that we often feel guilty as a result. Romans 3:11-23 is a litany of Old Testament passages emphasizing human failure. We may not all be guilty of all sins mentioned there, but we all fail at this point or that.

This failure leads to two observations. First, the desire to atone for or cover faults is the basis of all religious sacrifice and ritual. What is unique about Christianity is not that it offers a strong moral code to follow—many religions have comparable standards—but that it provides a single finished atonement for all failures to live up to such standards. Second, the Bible claims that humans are condemned not because they have not heard about Christ but because they have failed to live up to his standard of righteousness (Rom 3:23), a standard to which their own hearts and the creation itself bear witness (see Rom 2:14-15 and 10:18). The Bible intimates that all will not be judged according to the same standard (Rom 2:6, 12 and Rev 20:11-12), but that all fail to live up to whatever light they have been given (Rom 1:21). Their rejection of righteousness is really a rejection of God.

Now let us notice what God has done for mankind. We cannot read the biblical record and escape its emphasis on God's just response to unrighteousness, often called his wrath. God is the destroyer of the wicked.

The Lord preserves all who love him;
but all the wicked he will destroy. (Ps 145:20)

But at the same time God has shown himself to be longsuffering, not willing that any should perish (2 Pet 3:9). This is why he dealt mercifully with Israel and sent Christ to save the wicked. From the announcement to the shepherds (Lk 2:10) and the proclamation of John the Baptist (Jn 1:29), it is clear that Jesus is the Savior who came to take away the world's sin. He did not come into the world to condemn the world—the law had already done that—but to provide an escape from God's wrath (see Jn 3:17). Christ's death is for the whole world (1 Jn 2:2), and he offers his salvation to all nations. This is the general call, as John Calvin terms it, by "which God invites all equally to himself through the outward preaching of the word—even to those to whom he holds it out as a savor of death, and as the occasion for severer condemnation" (Institutes, III, xxiv, 8). God does not desire the death of sinners and his offer of salvation is for all, but those who reject it he will exclude from his presence.

God's eventual division of humanity is embarrassingly prominent in the preaching of Jesus; no one speaks more about hell than he does. Listen to his pronouncement in Luke 12:51: "Do you think that I have come to give peace on earth? No, I tell you, but rather division." He pictures judgment as a casting into the lake of fire. But notice that this place of suffering is not prepared for humanity but for the devil and his angels (Mt 25:41). People who reject God and his standards are made to share this fate. The book of Revelation warns: "If any one's name was not found written in the book of life, he was thrown into the lake of fire" (Rev 20:15).

We have said that those who reject the offer of salvation will be excluded from God's presence (though we do not know all that this exclusion will mean). Does this mean that those who have never heard the gospel may find some other way of coming to

God? The Bible clearly teaches that all people on the one hand have a knowledge of goodness mediated through nature and conscience, but that on the other hand all fail to achieve a standard of righteousness that is acceptable to God (Rom 1:18-21; 2:13-16). In rejecting righteousness they are rejecting God. It is not because they have not heard the gospel that they are condemned but because they reject the righteousness they already know. If they subsequently reject the gospel, it will be another expression of their fundamental disobedience. The preaching of the gospel is the means of salvation, not the cause of judgment (Jn 3:17).

Having said this we may make two qualifications. First, while all know something of righteousness, some know more than others. Thus we should leave open the possibility that judgment will be relative to knowledge and to obedience (Rom 2:12-15). Second, Strong suggests the possibility that, while all people fail to live up to God's standard, some may find grace by throwing themselves on God's mercy insofar as they know it. We cannot exclude the possibility that God's mercy is mediated through the fallen creation, though we may wonder to what extent this can happen. If anything is clear from the New Testament descriptions of heaven, it is the surprise that people will show at who is present (Mt 8:11-12). Since it is God's feast, he alone prepares the guest list. For our part, we should avoid either forming a rationalistic syllogism that moves directly from God's love to the salvation of all or speculating overmuch about the nature and objects of God's judgment. But that there is judgment, and that it is final and eternal, we are not free to doubt.

What is at stake in this teaching about judgment? We acknowledge a certain awkward reluctance to speak of it. In fact, the common reaction of Christians to this teaching is sorrow. Luther said that when he contemplated this destiny, he wished he had not been born. As Anthony Hoekema says, "We shall speak about hell with reluctance, with grief, perhaps even with tears—but speak about it we must" (p. 273. For we are not at liberty to change the teaching of Christianity to fit some modern form of consciousness. We accept it not because it pleases us, not because rejecting it would take the heart out of our missionary work, but because we believe it is what the Bible teaches.

What is at stake is God's claim to sovereignty. Christians who believe in final judgment are sometimes accused of being judgmental. But allowing God the final vindication of his righteousness is not the same thing as arrogating to oneself the role of judge. Indeed the Scriptures make clear that we are not to anticipate God's evaluation—we cannot say with certainty in any given case what God's judgment will be. We must leave judgment to God. As F. Wendel summarizes Calvin's view: "We have not to make ourselves the executors of the judgments that we may attribute with more or less probability to God. Predestination will be fully revealed to us only in the life beyond" (p. 284).

Or Christians are sometimes asked: If people will be condemned, then how can any Christian rest and enjoy life while many are dying in their sins? Here we may respond that God calls us to be responsible to our own gifts and callings, not to bear the burden of the world on our shoulders. We are to seek to extend God's kingdom where we are, with the means available to us; we are not asked to win its battles everywhere.

In all discussion of judgment something fundamental is at stake about the nature of God, the nature of humanity, and the relationship the Creator desires with his creation. The Christian faith insists that people live in a moral world where personal response and moral choice are necessary to being human. Caring for creation and our brothers and sisters is a moral responsibility we cannot evade. Our choices moreover reflect and grow out of our personal response to God and his revelation, a response now focusing on the lordship of Jesus Christ. Moral failure inevitably destroys our relation with God and consequently with the world. It cannot simply be overlooked, for left unchecked it would destroy not only the individual but also the world. Atonement must be made and relationships restored. Dealing with moral failure is necessary not only to the character of God but to human nature and to creation as well. If final judgment were simply removed, not only would moral seriousness and freedom of choice be destroyed, but the world itself would be altered. Our relationship with God would be moved out of the personal sphere in which Scripture places it and changed into a predetermined process. The whole carefully directed program of salvation would be unnecessary. All God's attempts to woo the human heart would be mere stage play and not the decisive events presented in the Bible.

It is true, as Barth pointed out, that Christ's victory is complete and will one day extend to all the created order. But this victory is no less complete for allowing a choice. People are still asked to decide whether to see Christ as Judge or as Lord. They may still, as Abraham Kuyper put it, cut themselves off from the root of humanity.

Syncretism

Whether or not we are troubled by the prospect of judgment, we may still wonder about the exclusivist claim of Christianity. Is personal knowledge of Christ the only way to God? This problem has accompanied Christianity from the beginning, but it has become acute only in modern times. Most people in the history of the world have lived and died in small cultural groupings having little or no contact with other cultures and religions. In our century modern transportation and communications systems have created an unprecedented interchange of people and ideas. Often so many ideas compete for our attention that we find it difficult to distinguish legitimate from spurious claims.

At the same time a romantic respect for individuality and natural dignity (beginning perhaps with the philosopher Rousseau) has fostered a tolerance for different points of view. After all, many people ask, isn't religion an individual or community matter? If it satisfies its adherents, why try to introduce a Christian viewpoint that might not work as well in that setting? Such questions reflect a new sociological perspective of religion wherein its function is more important than its truth. But they also reflect positive values of individual dignity and human freedom to think and act. The damage done to these liberties by totalitarian regimes has become all too clear in our generation.

Another factor has stimulated today's dislike of Christian exclusivism: the rise of nationalism. Peoples around the world have
a new (and often healthy) respect for their own local traditions.
We have our own religious and artistic traditions, people say;
why should we give these up? Are not all human traditions of
equal weight? Are they not all windows to let in God's light?

Romanticism, the human sciences and nationalism have all led
to what John R. W. Stott has called "fruit-cocktail religion."
Commonly we call this challenge *syncretism:* any form of religion
in which elements from more than one religious tradition are
combined. Various bridges, or areas of common ground, have
been suggested as places where people from various religions can
get together and understand each other. All religions have common elements which may be featured in our new, modern understanding of each other. Let us note some of these elements and
then point out ways in which Christianity is unique and may not
be compared with any other religion.

It is sometimes claimed that *morality* can unite us. All cultures
have moral standards that may provide a basis for some kind of
universally acceptable law. For example, truth-telling is everywhere revered:

A sacrifice is obliterated by a lie and the merit of alms by an act
of fraud. (Hindu. Janet, 1, 6)

The Master said, Be of unwavering good faith. (Ancient Chinese Analects, viii, 13)

The gentleman must learn to be faithful to his superior and to
keep promises. (Analects, 1, 8)

You shall not bear false witness against your neighbor. (Ex 20:16)

With few exceptions—the ideal of treachery among the Sawi
people mentioned earlier may be one—people universally recognize and submit themselves to norms such as speaking the truth

and refraining from murder. The question then arises, Why have dispute and warring characterized human history?

Some respond that we have not followed our essential human nature, which is basically good. These seek harmony by focusing on the *goodness and value of man*. In the third century B. C., Mencius said:

> If we follow our essential character we will be able to do good. This is what I mean in saying that man's nature is good. If man does evil, it is not the fault of his original endowment. . . . Therefore it is said: Seek and you will find them (love, righteousness, propriety and wisdom), neglect and you will lose them. (Quoted in Mercado, p. 180)

Thus by developing, through education and coordinated public policy, the values inherent in humanity, it should be possible to produce a good community.

But people do deviate from community norms. How will such lawbreakers be judged? Some claim that a *natural system of moral cause and effect* will "punish" evildoers. An example of this belief is the Hindu doctrine of karma, the cosmic law of destiny or moral causality. The Hindu goal is to renounce desire or to surrender totally to God's grace so as to find release from the eternal cycle of death and rebirth. The Hindu does not want to be "born again"! One Catholic writer suggested that karma is close to the biblical picture of reaping what one sows and so is a belief that Christians share with Hindus (Mercado, p. 185).

Another element common to all religions is *faith in God*. For most people in the non-Western world, faith in the supernatural is intuitive and spontaneous. Can this unite us? In Hinduism God is identified with the Brahman, the impersonal, all-pervading force of the universe. From time to time incarnations of the Brahman called avatars can lead us to enlightenment. The Buddha and Krishna are avatars, and many Hindus are willing to grant this exalted status to Christ. Why cannot there be more than one such revelation sent from God to lead men and women from a life of desire and illusion to one of spiritual union with him? Isn't such union after all the goal of Christ's ministry?

Because for many people these are important questions, they deserve careful consideration and discussion. Before making specific responses we may dispose of a number of improper criteria for judging the value of religious traditions. We cannot judge by the sincerity of the believers, for we all know of cases where people are both sincere and mistaken. We cannot judge by the age of the tradition. The oldest belief is not necessarily the most correct; neither is a belief wrong just because of old age (we cannot assume that newer views, being more scientific, are thereby more accurate). We cannot judge by the beauty of a tradition. Mistaken religious traditions have sometimes produced much religious art, but we must not mistake beauty for truth. Finally we cannot judge by the number of adherents. People are often impressed by the size of a religious tradition, as if so many folk could hardly be wrong. A moment's thought, however, will correct this error: how often prophets or geniuses have been persecuted by the majority simply because they dared insist on unpopular truth! Truth cannot be determined by vote.

Nor may we avoid the question of truth by moving to a higher level of generality. A prominent attempt along this line was made not long ago by John Hick. He proposed that rather than placing Christianity (or some other faith) in the center of our thinking, we have a Copernican revolution and realize "that it is God who is at the centre, and that all the religions of mankind, including our own, serve and revolve around him" (1973b, p. 131). He believes he is giving up a confessional stance for a nondogmatic approach. But in actuality he is not giving up commitment to a particular religion so much as replacing faith in some traditional creed with faith in his own concept of God. In asking us to accept his concept of God, which as Lesslie Newbigin points out only a few philosophers will be able to grasp, Hick does less than justice not only to the truth-claims of Christianity but also to those of any other faith (see Newbigin, pp. 184-89). Moreover by refusing to place his concept on a level with other faiths, he makes impossible any meeting among people of different faiths. Truth seekers must give up their dogmas and join him in his realization of God, he seems to say, for he alone has awakened from dogmatic slumbers. The truth question and Christianity's claim of uniqueness cannot be so easily avoided

One further caution. Christians sometimes feel that because of the uniqueness of their faith they must deny all value to human reflection about God outside revelation. That Christianity is unique does not mean it always contradicts the rest of human thinking. Christianity in its emphasis on creation and common grace recognizes that since God rules over the nations, there is at least a dim awareness of his truth everywhere. How then does Christianity respond to the sense of morality everywhere? To man's faith in himself? To his sense of justice and his belief in God?

First, why cannot Christians unite with non-Christians who share our moral standards? Because Christianity is not based on morality. The Bible does not pretend to contain all that is worthwhile in the area of morals. What makes religion necessary is not the presence or absence of moral laws but the failure of people to keep these standards. What the Bible presents is not only a system of laws—some of these can be found elsewhere—but primarily a series of historical events through which God is said to be actively reconciling humanity to himself, overcoming human failure by his own strength and goodness and establishing a new community. Other religions have myths about dying gods and the resurrection of life in the spring, but it is Christianity's unique claim that God became an actual man who demonstrated the reality of God's love and power, died a sacrificial death and rose again. Christ is not an avatar pointing people toward God; he is the God-man who actually brings about reconciliation between God and man. The Bible claims to record the saving events—from the Exodus to the cross and the consummation—that alone constitute the avenue whereby man may come to know and fellowship with God. These events, not merely a system of moral ideas, have changed the course of history and determined human progress.

Second, why cannot all sincerely held beliefs be equally valid? Because often claims are mutually exclusive. We would not insist that one medicine is as good as another so long as the patient is sincere, and that each person may make up his own mind on the matter. Mencius said that "man's nature is good." His claim directly contradicts Christ's statement: "What comes out of a man is what defiles a man. For from within, out of the heart of man, come evil thoughts, fornication, theft, murder, adultery. . . . All these evil things come from within, and they defile a man" (Mk 7:20-23). Whom are we to believe? Christianity recognizes that human nature as God created it was good, but that it is now perverted: not that people cannot do good things—this is obviously untrue—but that they cannot help doing evil things. It seems that Christianity realistically assesses human capabilities and clearly contradicts other religious claims at this point.

Third, why can we not base a world religion on our common respect for justice? Because Christianity does not agree with other religions about how this justice relates to human history.

Christians claim that because of the death and resurrection of Christ, the kingdom of heaven can begin to be experienced in this order of time and space. In Hindu and Buddhist views of salvation the goal is escape from this temporal order. Thus there can be no impetus to improve the lot of people in this life, especially when it is believed to be determined by behavior in a previous life. By contrast Marxist-Leninist views of salvation look forward to an entirely this-worldly fulfillment of human hopes; they leave out the transcendent dimension entirely. Christian salvation effects genuine reconciliation among people and calls believers to be salt and light in their communities even while remembering that their citizenship is in heaven where they will enjoy eternal fellowship with God. Christianity endows this life with new moral seriousness. The Christ event calls for a decision by all exposed to it and anticipates a judgment of all human activities. Now all of life—and thus all of human history—must be seen in the light shed by Christ's death, his resurrection and his promised return. Thus the uniqueness of the Christian claim rests not on philosophical premises but on past, present and future events which demand that human beings live responsibly in God's presence.

Fourth, why is it not possible for people to unite around a common faith in God? Because only Christianity provides assured access to God. Of course it is God's purpose to unite his creation in common worship; the Scriptures imply that this was his ultimate reason for creating the universe. It is also true that faith in God is a basic need of human nature. Indeed theoretical atheism is unknown in the Old Testament (the fool who denies God in Ps 14:1 is not doubting his existence but refusing to acknowledge God's claims over his life), just as it is very uncommon in the non-Western (and non-Communist) world today.

Scholars of comparative religion are beginning to think that belief in one God was the original view, obscured and overladen in the course of time by magic, animism and polytheism (Anderson, 1970, p. 75). In the Philippines, for example, many believe in a great and distant god called Bathala. But this god is believed to be so distant that one must appeal to lesser deities as intermediaries to reach him. The problem is not a failure to believe that God exists, but the inability to have significant contact with him. How can I know God and be assured that he is favorably disposed toward me? At this point the Christian answer parts company with all others. The Christian view of revelation is unique. The idea of revelation or disclosure in itself is not unique to Christianity. Different religions have gods who speak through dreams, special prophets or holy men. But Jesus Christ is not a prophet speaking a word about God or relating visions of God's will seen in dreams. Jesus is God himself come down to the level of everyday human life, sharing its joys and sorrows and expressing in concrete terms his very character. We have so often heard this that we tend to overlook its staggering implications. Jesus is not a message from God; he is God himself in the flesh of human existence. The fact of this claim lies at the center of Jesus' ministry. E. O. James said: "The Godhead attributed to the founder of Christianity . . . renders it unique in the history of religion. Nowhere else has it ever been claimed that a historical founder of any religion was the one and only supreme deity" (quoted in Anderson, 1970, p. 92). In the Gospel account, hardly a day went by in Christ's ministry that he did not take to himself some privilege reserved for God alone: he forgave sins, he raised the dead, he calmed the sea; he claimed to be "the bread of life," "the light of the world," "the door," "the good shepherd" (Jn 6:35; 8:12; 10:9, 11). He capped his claims by asserting: "No one knows the Son except the Father, and no one knows the Father except the Son and any one to whom the Son chooses to reveal him" (Mt 11:27), and "I am the way, and the truth, and the life; no one comes to the Father, but by me" (Jn 14:6). Some insist that Jesus never said these things, but even critical New Testament scholars admit that these sayings appear in the most primitive level of the writings. One cannot extract a merely human Jesus from the Gospels. Or it could be that Jesus was mistaken about himself, that he made exaggerated or completely false claims. But Jesus' character is so consistently good, his behavior so lacking in lunatic traits, that few have argued along those lines. Either his claim is false or, as Stephen Neill insists, it casts the shadow of falsehood on every other system. Neill asserts:

This Christian claim is naturally offensive to the adherents of every other religious system. It is almost as offensive to modern man, brought up in the atmosphere of relativism, in which tolerance is regarded almost as the highest of the virtues. But we must not suppose that this claim to universal validity is something that can quietly be removed from the Gospel without changing it into something entirely different from what it is. The mission of Jesus was limited to the Jews and did not look immediately beyond them; but his life, his method and his message do not make sense, unless they are interpreted in the light of his own conviction that he was in fact the final and decisive word of God to men. . . . For the human sickness there is one specific remedy, and this is it. There is no other. (pp. 16-17)

The dimensions of Christ's claim and the scope of the redemption he inaugurated are such that the fragments of truth found in other religions are insignificant by comparison. Of course they are not valueless; God often uses our halting and inadequate knowledge to help us understand higher things. But to combine Christian truth with insights gleaned from other religions is out of the question. To be sure, we must express truth in terms of our own place and time. We may freely draw analogies from the religious experience of the people we serve. But the truth is we are confronted by God's special call only in Christ. The heart of our work will always be proclaiming the shattering news of Christ's death and resurrection, for this is the source of the stream that God intends to use to water all the parched and thirsty nations. At times, bewildered at the concentration of such importance in those few years of Palestinian history, we wonder how this can be so. We may well be amazed, for amazement is at the heart of worship; we are not free to change the message, for that is to disbelieve. As Evelyn Underhill has written: "If the reality of God were small enough to be grasped, it would not be great enough to be adored; and so our holiest privilege would go."

Questions for Review

1. Compare the views of A. H. Strong and Paul Tillich on universalism.
2. On what basis are men and women judged and separated from God?
3. How is the character of God at stake in judgment?
4. How could universalism affect one's view of individual responsibility?
5. List three reasons that syncretism is attractive today.
6. What bridges have been suggested to unite people in religion?
7. How is the Christian view of history unique?
8. How is the Christian view of human nature unique?
9. How is the Christian view of salvation unique?
10. What claims does Christ make for himself? How does this relate to the Hindu concept of *avatar*?
11. Why cannot a common faith in God unite people?

CHAPTER SEVEN

The Empirical Sciences

We turn now to the challenge offered by the sciences, both empirical and social. It is possible to argue that Christianity and the sciences ought to be allies rather than adversaries. For on the one hand, the Christian view of the person and creation lies behind the development of modern science. On the other hand, a direct confrontation between Christianity and the sciences should be impossible because of their different methods and subject matter. Though we cannot argue this latter point in any detail, we will seek to show that these two perspectives on reality are complementary rather than contradictory. The fact that Christians are called on to "reconcile" their faith with science may be best accounted for historically rather than philosophically.

Historically the church has, officially and unofficially, taken stands against scientific hypotheses. One thinks of the Reformers' attack on Copernican views and the confrontation between Galileo and the Roman Church. But we should not overlook the fact that a majority of the early scientific pioneers were Christians who believed their work to be consistent expressions of their Christian convictions. Although few twentieth-century scientists profess any religions conviction, this may not be due so much to a conscious rejection of Christian teaching as to an acquiescence to the general secular framework in which they are trained. The long and bitter debate between creationists and evolutionists has only served to increase a sense of confrontation rather than to encourage mutual understanding.

In this chapter we will mediate this conflict in two ways. First we will point out the need for a conceptual framework in which to do science, and second we will show Christianity's contribution to habits of thought congenial to the rise of modern science. Following this we will look at specific problem areas where Christian faith and scientific hypothesis need not conflict. We will conclude by describing one model that may help clarify the relation between science and Christianity.

Christianity and the Rise of Modern Science

Scientists were once expected to approach their subjects in a perfectly objective way, without preconceived ideas, and simply observe whatever was there. It is now clear that science does not and indeed cannot proceed in such a fashion. Rather if scientists are to *see* something they must have some idea of what they are looking for. Thomas Kuhn calls a set of ideas in terms of which scientists work a *paradigm*. According to Kuhn, scientists do their work with a mental set that includes theory and some application, is fruitful in suggesting further research and is widely accepted in the profession. Paradigms are not fixed; indeed they are widely questioned by scientists just before a scientific revolution (as in the closing years of the nineteenth century, just before the formulation of the theory of relativity). Kuhn's use of paradigm has been criticized as ambiguous, but one can no longer doubt that scientific dogma plays an essential part in doing what Kuhn calls "normal science."

This may be illustrated by sketching in three world models that scientists have used to guide their scientific research and which have shown Christian influence. We can do no more here than outline the issues involved and encourage the interested student to pursue the matter independently.

The first model, developed and articulated during the Middle Ages, may be called the *organic model*. It sees the world as an organism, a living and ordered unity. R. Hooykaas believes that Greek rationalism and the biblical world picture both contributed to this model. The Greek emphasis on mathematics, logic and methods of observation laid the groundwork for what we call today the experimental method. Christianity contributed the idea that the world was an ordered structure in which God could intervene supernaturally but which ordinarily ran according to natural laws. Though we now recognize this model's limitations, it enabled us to find out a great deal about the world. In many ways it was a comfortable picture. The world and man were the focus of the universe, the heavens were alive with light and music, and people sought within nature for the secret of wealth and happiness (through, for example, alchemy and the search for the fountain of youth).

Although there were Christian elements in this model, there were also elements incompatible with a Christian perspective. Whereas the Greeks—and their medieval followers—insisted that the world has divine characteristics, the Bible proclaimed that God and the world are separate. Whereas the Greeks believed reason was more important than experience (and thus rational constructions truer than observed reality), the Bible demonstrated that knowledge usually comes through experience (a posteriori). Just as we cannot say in advance how God will save his people, so we cannot perfectly predict how nature will act. We must allow facts to come to us as a kind of revelation (see Hooykaas, p. 44). Finally, whereas the Greeks insisted that man cannot equal nature, the Bible instructed man to control and subdue the created order.

This biblical perspective helped pave the way for the scientific revolutions that were coming. Alfred North Whitehead in his study of the rise of modern science asserts: "Faith in the possibility of science, generated antecedently to the development of modern scientific theory, is an unconscious derivative from medieval theology" (p. 19). Statements by those involved in this revolution indicating their Christian perspective support the idea of a connection between science and theology. For example, Copernicus expressed his annoyance that philosophers "had discovered no sure scheme for the movements of the machinery of the world, which has been built by the Best and most orderly Workman of all" (quoted in MacKay, 1965, p. 14). It is hardly possible to see his work toward a heliocentric universe as a revolt against his Christian principles.

Other factors also played a vital role in stimulating desire for a new way of looking at the world: factors such as the development of mathematics, a discipline preserved in the Arab world during the Middle Ages, and the widening of horizons occasioned by voyages of discovery.

In the seventeenth century Galileo and Newton led in shaping what is now called the *mechanistic model* of the world. Emphasis on observation and quantity led to a point of view that supposed the world to be a kind of machine. If the Middle Ages saw the world primarily in qualitative terms, the world now was understood primarily quantitatively, as a mechanical system of forces and material points. Space is an absolute receptacle in which this system eternally operates.

Because this model is so completely out of fashion today, it may be hard for us to appreciate the advance it represents over the previous model. The world was with one stroke demythologized and thus opened up for human exploration. If the world is the work of a good and ordered intelligence, we can explore it confident that it will yield its secrets to our patient research. Moreover advances in mathematics made it possible to describe and predict behavior of objects in a very exact way. Christians soon were comparing the world with a giant clock wound up by God.

From a Christian point of view, however, this model had problems that were not initially appreciated. While in the Middle Ages all events were understood in terms of their purpose in God's program, now it was tempting to place God at the beginning of an otherwise purely mechanical causal order. He may have put the machine in motion in the first place, but we hardly need his presence once things are working properly. After all, the clock can work very well after the clockmaker has gone home. The French astronomer and mathematician Laplace (1749-1827) was asked why he gave so little place to God in his work. He responded with an epigram that has become famous: "Sire, I have no need of that hypothesis." (Interestingly, Laplace would certainly have claimed to be a Christian.)

Another problem with the mechanistic model was also serious, not only from a theistic but also from a humanistic standpoint. The place for humanity and human values in the scheme of things was severely reduced, and the universe became a cold, unfeeling environment. The person seemed to be reduced to a chance and temporary product of primary forces without final purpose or meaning. Ironically, a Christian who considered his devotional writings more significant than his scientific work, Sir Isaac Newton, did the most to frame this world view leaving so little room for either God or humanity. E. A. Burtt notes:

> The great Newton's authority was squarely behind that view of the cosmos which saw in man a puny irrelevant spectator . . . of the vast mathematical system whose regular motions according to mechanical principles constituted the world of nature. The gloriously romantic universe of Dante . . . had been swept away. . . . The world that people had thought themselves living in—a world rich with color and sound, redolent with fragrance, filled with gladness, love and beauty, speaking everywhere of purposive harmony and creative ideals—was crowded now into minute corners in the brains of scattered organic beings. The really important world outside was a world hard, cold, colorless, silent and dead. (pp. 238-39)

This sorry state of affairs seemed to threaten more than the Christian religion; it bode ill for all human values. Antireligious zealots nonetheless noisily announced the demise of religion and the arrival of scientific truth as though this were a matter for rejoicing. French philosophers during the Enlightenment were eager to use science as a weapon against religion. An extremely influential book at the end of the nineteenth century was *Force and Matter* by Ludwig Buchner, who dogmatized that the indestructibility or permanence of matter was a firmly established scientific fact. The universe, he concluded, must therefore be uncreated. Barely ten years later, Buchner's thesis was completely disproved.

While Buchner's book was avidly being read by people anxious for the certainties of science (it went through more than twenty printings), a deep-seated malaise among serious scientists was preparing the way for a revolution to an entirely new world model. Experiments were not giving the expected results. Some daring individuals began to wonder whether the whole framework was mistaken. Some began to ask whether scientists' quantitative emphasis resulted from asking only quantitative questions. If force and matter are all that your paradigm allows you to see, you should not be resentful if they are all that you find. But quantitative questions are not necessarily the only questions that may be asked.

With Albert Einstein's formulation of the general and special theories of relativity, a new scientific framework was suggested. We may call it the *energistic model*. Whereas matter and forces were absolute and discrete in the former model, Einstein suggested that motion is relative to the system of forces in which it takes place. On this premise, our conceptions of place and time are only fictions useful because we ordinarily work on a small scale. Whereas earlier scientists thought of the universe as a receptacle in which objects move, we now look at it as a field of interrelated forces. Objects therefore do not have absolute identity but can be defined only relative to given situations. Ideas of movement and rest are in one sense conventions used to make sense of experience. Even objects can be understood in terms of more than one perspective: light may be understood as either a wave or a particle; gas may be discrete particles or a continuous medium. Bertrand Russell describes how difficult it is to form a mental picture of this model: "Suppose all the houses in London were perpetually moving about, like a swarm of bees; suppose railways moved and changed shape like avalanches; and finally suppose material objects were perpetually being formed and dissolved like clouds" (1969, pp. 11-12).

Some have thought that the energistic model results in the view that there are no absolutes and that everything is relative. Whatever popularizers have claimed, the model as scientists understand it has quite the opposite intention. As Russell notes, the theory of relativity "is wholly concerned to exclude what is relative and arrive at a statement of physical laws that shall in no way depend upon the circumstances of the observer" (1969, p. 16). Philosophically, then, this model of the world poses no threat to Christianity. As a paradigm, or set of hypotheses that account for empirical facts, it makes no claim to ultimate status. In fact, scientists today tend to be very cautious in their statements about the status of scientific models. The World Book article on the theory of relativity comments that scientific theories do not claim finality: "The relativity theory, like all our theories, is an invention of the human mind. New theories may eventually show limitations of the relativity theory and deal with problems that the relativity theory does not cover." Moreover science cannot pretend to answer questions that are not verifiable by its methods. It is perfectly reasonable to understand the orderly working of what we call natural laws as an expression of God's providence. Indeed if providence is rejected, it must be replaced with an equally comprehensive framework in which science has meaning.

It can even be argued that this latest model for understanding the world provides less of a challenge to Christianity than any previous model. The dynamic and energistic dimensions of reality are now clearly recognized and seem to provide "elbow room" —to use E. L. Mascall's phrase—for a Christian interpretation of reality. T. F. Torrance, in fact, argues that this new model rests on ideas deriving from a Christian understanding of the relation of God to the universe, so that if we interpret our Christian faith within the patterns of this new paradigm, "we find that our basic Christian convictions are clarified and fortified and are given an even deeper relevance to the exciting world that daily opens to our scientific inquiries" (p. 145). Even problem areas can prepare the way for the Christian claim that the Christian perspective best accounts for observable reality.

Potential Tension Areas between Christianity and Science
Centrality of humanity. In the Middle Ages it was easy to believe in the importance of God's program of redemption, for all the universe was believed to revolve around the earth. Modern astronomy gives no such distinguished place to our planet and even holds out the possibility—much discussed these days—of intelligent life on other planets. Is it naive vanity to see the earth as the focal point of God's redemptive program?

The existence or nonexistence of life on other planets does not affect the fact that sin and redemption are possible on our planet. God's visit to this planet does not preclude the possibility of his interest in other planets. The modest place accorded the earth is in fact perfectly consistent with the theocentric character of Christianity. In the Christian view the focus of events is not the person or the earth but God. All that exists has been created to glorify him, and therefore neither humankind nor the earth need occupy the central place in the universal scheme of things.

Although the earth is an object of God's special attention, as Romans 8:19-21 and Ephesians 1:10 make clear, there is no reason to think that it is alone in having his attention. At the same time there is growing evidence that natural processes are correlated with human existence so as to make the universe a suitable home for humanity. It appears, for example, that the universe had to expand precisely as it did for life to emerge, as though, in the words of J. A. Wheeler, "the universe had to adapt itself from its earliest days to the future requirements for life and mind" (quoted in Torrance, p. 140).

Resurrection and immortality. Some scientists contend that current definitions of mind make it impossible to believe that an immaterial mind can survive death. Human intelligence and consciousness are widely believed to depend on physical states. How can a person survive death and exist in some nonbodily state in the presence of God?

Far from disproving Christianity, these scientists confirm one of its central teachings: human hope lies in the bodily resurrection of the dead and not in immortality. Moreover resurrection, according to biblical teaching, is a part of God's renewing and restoring of the whole created order. The Christian hope is not in survival but in translation into a new order of existence, a wholly new physical system. Mascall comments: "Because we are by our nature physical beings, linked by our bodily metabolism both with one another and with the rest of the material world, our resurrection will involve nothing less than the transformation of the whole material order" (1965, p. 17).

Of course we have problems conceptualizing this transformation. How will the resurrection body be the same person? But personal identity is a mystery even during our lifetime; we are physically different persons every seven years. Indeed the dynamic understanding of matter makes identity a convention. Continuity is found in the process and interrelationship of situations, not necessarily in identical physical particles. And what about the so-called intermediate state? It may involve some temporary conscious state in God's presence that we cannot now comprehend. In the biblical view it is at best a temporary unstable condition, a waiting to be further clothed (2 Cor 5:1-5).

Location of heaven. Christianity is often criticized for its tendency to locate heaven in some physical place in the universe. With our relative notion of place, where could heaven be?

Heaven's location was more of a problem when space was considered a receptacle against which all movement could be measured and in which every object must be located. Now we prefer to think of different (but related) systems to which space and time are relative. As Mascall notes: "It is no longer necessary to hold that all experiences which involve spatial characteristics must be linked together in one unified extensional spatial continuum" (1965, p. 28). If locating heaven is a problem, the fault may lie more with our imagination than with Christian truth. This is not a surprise to the believer who hears Paul (quoting the prophet Isaiah): " 'What no eye has seen, nor ear heard, nor the heart of man conceived, what God has prepared for those who love him,' God has revealed to us through the Spirit" (1 Cor 2:9-10).

A personal God. Some argue that the modern understanding of the interrelated character of reality leaves little room for the intervention of a personal God. Albert Einstein, who was no opponent of religion in general, once said:

> The main source of the present-day conflicts between the spheres of religion and science lies in this concept of a personal God. . . . The more a man is imbued with the ordered regularity of all events the firmer becomes his conviction that there is no room left by the side of this ordered regularity for causes of a different nature. (pp. 27-28)

But as Einstein goes on to recognize, allowing for a personal God is no different in principle from allowing for human purposes and creativity within the natural system of cause and effect. The assumption of universal causality—the belief that every event has an anterior cause—can be a legitimate methodological tool. But it does not follow that universal causality is the only frame of reference within which the world may be understood. Other dimensions must be allowed not only to account for divine causality but also to make room for human meaning in general.

Evolution. One of the most celebrated encounters between Christianity and science began when Charles Darwin published his famous book, *On the Origin of Species.* Many Christians took his view of the natural development of living forms to be a challenge to the biblical teaching that God created people and animals by a direct act. The issue is important, and more than a century later the discussion shows no signs of letting up, but many Christians today are convinced that the teaching of evolution—whatever its truth or falsity—does not directly threaten Christianity.

Let us see why this is so.

First, the teaching of evolution by its major exponents is not so dogmatic as sometimes pictured by the popularizers. It is true that most university biologists believe that evolution is the best understanding of development and that the theory has become scientific orthodoxy. But partly because they recognize the role that paradigms play in scientific inquiry and partly because they lack certain corroborative evidence, scientists often show caution in their pronouncements. It is helpful to remember that evolution cannot directly challenge religion because it, like all scientific hypotheses, does not claim to be certain. It is a probability statement that gathers together various generalizations about the obvious role of process and development in the order of things. The best scientists recognize the problems facing the theory: the mechanism of evolution is still unclear; fundamental energy processes in the universe appear disintegrative; and offspring generally keep within a limited range of variability (and so expected transitional forms are often missing). For most biologists, however, the theory remains the most satisfying explanation for the development of complex forms.

Second, we should recognize that the Genesis account itself cannot settle scientific questions of development. Time indications, for example, are notably absent from the account (unless "evening and morning" are understood to refer to a literal twenty-four-hour day, but this is not required by the context). In fact some have concluded that the phrase "let the earth bring forth" in Genesis 1 implies that God used natural (evolutionary) processes in creation. This view, sometimes called theistic evolution, holds that God originated and directed the process but that he used natural causes to accomplish his purposes. This is perhaps a minority view among Christians, but it does indicate the interpretations that these verses have been subject to. Most Christians insist that this phrase is a metaphoric way of speaking of God's direct and intimate work of creation, though it may still have taken place progressively over long periods of time. Divergent views among Christians show that the Genesis material by itself cannot provide a definitive scientific theory. Christians—or the biologists among them—are still called upon to provide an alternative interpretive theory that can be harmonized both with observable facts and with Genesis.

Clearly either creationism or evolutionism as a scientific theory calls for a larger framework in which it can be understood. Obviously many evolutionists are also naturalists who believe the universe resulted from chance and accidental processes. They insist that matter possesses some quality that makes evolution possible. Such an assumption of an unobserved quality is no more nor less an act of faith than the view that a personal Creator made the world from no previously existing material. Both are assumptions that cannot be tested scientifically.

A larger framework is also needed to deal with the question of final meaning or purpose. The evolutionary theory by itself cannot provide meaning for the universe. One must either deny that such meaning exists or seek it in some religious or philosophical framework. Finally, a larger framework must settle the question of origins. Did the process begin by a chance collocation of eternal matter, or was it created by a personal and eternal God? Christians can be confident that nothing in the scientific view necessarily denies an intelligence at work forming the natural universe, and much evidence supports such a view.

The Relation between Christianity and Science

We have seen that modern views on the nature of reality need offer little direct challenge to Christian belief. As Einstein insisted, "Science without religion is lame, religion without science is blind" (p. 26). We must be careful, however, not to insist that modern science and Christianity are directly correlated. Someone has wisely said that to marry theology with the science of one generation is to risk leaving theology a widow in the next. This is not because scientific theories threaten to disprove Christianity, but because it lies outside the scope of genuine science to come to the aid of any religious theory. Scientists themselves need some ultimate framework to provide meaning and purpose for their activities, be it Christianity, naturalism or Marxism. For their part, Christians should be careful what support they accept for the truth of their faith. Often enough we have seen an argument marshaled in support of Christianity turn into a double-edged sword. If we are fully Christian in our thinking, God is at the center and not the periphery of our thoughts. He is the beginning and not the end of our arguments.

All of this suggests how we should make use of the Bible in our discussions about science. As Christians we stand humbly before the facts. God did not give the Bible to make scientific work unnecessary. He gave it to help us develop a total perspective in which science has meaning. Moreover biblical language is not scientific; it shows God's accommodation to popular human thought and expression. The Bible communicates God's truth to common people in everyday language. Its statements about nature are not systematized or intended to give complete explanations of the physical world. But they do suggest how it should be approached: with careful, loving observation (as Christ seems to have watched the birds and flowers), with confidence in its order and goodness, but with recognition of its ultimate dependence on God. This does not make scientific study unnecessary; in fact, it encourages it. Most important the Bible makes possible a philosophy of science that relates all God's works to their source and points them to their end.

What then is the relation between religious faith and science? Some have suggested that religion issues in personal knowledge while science leads to objective knowledge. Gordon Clark (1964) suggests the view of science which he calls *operationalism:* A concept is equal to the corresponding set of operations used to determine the concept. Science provides methods of utilizing nature, while religion provides values and goals for these operations. The most helpful model I have seen comes from British cyberneticist and information theorist D. M. MacKay (1957), who calls his view *complementarity.* He believes that science and religion give complementary rather than competing views of the same phenomena. The difference is analogous to the different functions of an actor and an observer in a drama. Science views man and nature from the outside, thus creating a distance between the object and observer. Religion, on the other hand, views the person as actor, taking part in the drama, immersed in the situation and responding to demands implicit in the circumstances. As an example the debate about determinism and free will may be approached in these terms. Determinism approaches the questions from the point of view of observer, free will as an actor in the drama. If we accept MacKay's metaphor we cannot join some of our forebears in seeing God as an absentee machine tender, for this would be to restrict him to the scientific half of the equation.

Indeed, from the religious point of view the universe may be like a thought rather than a machine, where purpose rather than mechanism permeates the order of things. (Such a formulation escapes the danger of a "God of the gaps" explanation which introduces religion whenever scientific answers are not forthcoming.) Of course no individual, whether scientist or Christian, is completely objective or totally involved. The actor and the spectator must be seen as aspects of the whole person which operate in mutual interrelationship, providing complementary perspectives. Neither point of view can be reduced to the other, and thus there need be no mutual suspicions. Both functions are part of the human call to reflect the image of the Creator and to fulfill the role of underlord in the created order.

T. F. Torrance (pp. 138-45) has further elaborated the idea of complementarity. He argues that there must be a correlation between the way we understand God's self-revelation and the way we progressively understand creation since, on Christian grounds, creation and redemption are ultimately interrelated in the purposes of God. The progressive understanding of the stratified levels of creation that is the product of scientific inquiry includes a thrust toward some intelligible end. This thrust has its correlation in the biblical understanding of God as creator and redeemer and in the final purposes he has for creation. This larger context, while it lies beyond the scope of scientific methods, provides the various levels of scientific understanding with a significance beyond what they are capable of in themselves; it completes (rather than negates) what they are in themselves. The miracles of the incarnation and resurrection then would break the symmetry of the lower levels of order with the symmetry of a higher level, taking up the dissonance into a profound reordering of the whole. Both MacKay and Torrance suggest that much remains to be learned from an intelligent conversation between the sciences and Christian theology. While we may still have to defend ourselves from attacks mounted from the scientific direction, we may be fully confident that there is no final or insurmountable conflict.

Questions for Review

1. List some historical reasons for the mistrust between science and religion.
2. Explain the difference between the mechanistic and organic world models.
3. How was the mechanistic model an improvement over the previous one? How was it dangerous to a Christian view?
4. What contributions did the biblical world picture make to the overthrow of the organic model?
5. Explain the energistic model. Why need it pose little threat to Christianity?
6. Does God's concern for humanity conflict with the findings of modern astronomy? Why or why not?
7. How do modern views allow room for resurrection and heaven?
8. Why should Christians be careful of seeking support from science?
9. Explain and defend the complementarity model of the relation between science and religion.

CHAPTER EIGHT

The Social Sciences

*T*he tensions between Christianity and the social sciences in many ways reflect the older conflicts with the empirical sciences. Certainly one of the most important attacks on Christianity in our generation is mounted by these younger (and brasher!) human sciences. In any case a great deal of mutual suspicion exists between Christianity and the social sciences. Christians sometimes think that God has told them in the Bible all they need to know about the world—the essential fact is that men and women are sinners—and that they need only get on with the job of spreading the gospel. Meanwhile social scientists often dismiss believers as closed-minded and prejudiced people blind to the real causes of their faith. Happily there are signs that this incomprehension is giving way to dialog. Christians are beginning to recognize that they cannot effectively serve God in a particular community without a basic knowledge of the structure and values of that community. Thus they are learning to appreciate the methods of the social sciences. For their part, social scientists are beginning to turn their attention to religion, and their recent studies have thrown valuable light on the relation between religious values and the societies in which they are found. Some such studies, to be sure, have produced results which put Christianity in an unfavorable light, but this only suggests that the real conflict is not between Christianity and the social sciences but between certain representatives of each group. It is our view that the two points of view need each other: Christians need to understand as much as possible about the world around them in order to bear an intelligent witness to Christ, while the social sciences need some larger framework to give meaning to their activities.

We will focus on psychology and sociology because their visibility makes them an insistent threat to Christian values, taking up the challenge begun over a hundred years ago by the empirical sciences. Turning first to the challenge offered by some psychologists, we will offer a Christian response. Then we will consider the challenge made by some sociologists.

Psychology

Psychology is the descriptive study of mental processes and human behavior. We will consider the challenge to Christianity posed by two eminent psychologists, Sigmund Freud (1856-1939) and B. F. Skinner (b. 1904).

Sigmund Freud. Freud, an heir of the nineteenth-century German idealist tradition and especially of the views of Ludwig Feuerbach, is a father of modern psychology and originator of one of its schools, psychoanalysis. In his essay *The Future of an Illusion* Freud claims that religion is merely the projection of human desires. He shapes this viewpoint into a formidable attack on the validity of Christianity. Freud believed that destructive, antisocial and anticultural drives present in all people tended to determine their behavior in society. Because instincts so often threaten to take precedence over intelligence, civilization defends itself against uncontrolled individual behavior by building institutions, particularly religious ones, which coerce individuals to renounce their instincts. Civilization protects humanity not only against itself but also against the terrors of nature: illness, catastrophe and death. It uses religion to provide comfort. Says Freud: "If the elements have passions that rage as they do in our own souls, if death itself is not something spontaneous but the violent act of an evil will, if everywhere in nature there are Beings around us of a kind that we know in our own society, then we can breathe freely, we can feel at home in the uncanny and can deal by psychical means with our senseless anxiety" (p. 22). Religion then is a defense mechanism against the terrors of both human and physical nature, a way to humanize the world. This humanization is the heart of Freud's view of religion. If we can make our fears into beings like us, we can associate with them as equals and appeal to them as, say, to a father. Freud points out that in personifying these elements, we are following an infantile model wherein the child seeks to influence people by establishing a relationship with them (p. 31).

Why do we insist on believing such fantasies? Because they fulfill the oldest, strongest and most urgent wish of humankind: our wish for immortality. "The prolongation of earthly existence in a future life provides the local and temporal framework in which these wish fulfillments take place" (pp. 47-48). The natural sciences inform us that none of this can be true. Moreover comparative research has shown the "fatal resemblance" between religious ideas and the thinking of primitive peoples: the primal father was the original image of God. The time then has come for us to remove the repression that religion brings about and to replace it with the rational operation of the intellect. People ought not to go on being children, Freud insists; they need to be educated to reality. For, he concludes, "by withdrawing their expectations from the other world and concentrating all their liberated energies into their life on earth, they will probably succeed in achieving a state of things in which life will become tolerable for everyone and civilization no longer oppressive to anyone" (p. 82).

Freud faces the objection that his solution may only be another kind of wish fulfillment. Can people really triumph over their instincts? He gives two reasons for thinking so. First, if he is wrong in hoping for a better world, it is not an argument for the truth of religion; indeed it would destroy the hope held out by religion as well. Second, he insists he is willing to change his views if science proves him wrong. He states his creed in these terms:

> We believe that it is possible for scientific work to gain some knowledge about the reality of the world, by means of which we can increase our power and in accordance with which we can arrange our life. If this belief is an illusion, then we are in the same position as you [believers in religion]. But science has given us evidence by its numerous and important successes that it is no illusion. (p. 90)

It is ironic that Freud should rest his faith in science as the ultimate hope of humankind, for it is from science that the strongest criticisms of his views have arisen. What Freud gives us, some critics claim, is not science at all but philosophical theory. His views of the "primal hoard" lying beneath culture are now generally rejected by anthropologists. A. L. Kroeber calls Freud's explanation of culture "intuitive, dogmatic, and wholly unhistorical" (Hick, 1973b, p. 35). Furthermore his atomistic and deterministic views of human culture are criticized as lacking empirical foundation. *The Future of an Illusion,* however, has been continuously kept in print and is still influential in its presentation of religion as a psychological crutch. Is the Christian faith an example of wish fulfillment? We must carefully consider this challenge.

Logically the question of whether Christianity is or is not wish fulfillment is separate from the question of God's existence or nonexistence. The fact that we wish for God and immortality does not prove they do not exist. Because a lonely person longs for the visit of a friend does not mean that an actual visit is merely wish fulfillment. As Freud seems to recognize, the charge of wish-fulfillment is two-edged: unbelief may also be wish fulfillment. Irrespective of our wishes on the matter, we still have to marshall our arguments for or against Christianity, for or against the existence of God.

Freud's view that people can achieve mastery of the intellect over instincts is more than a scientific hypothesis; it is a philosophical statement whose validity depends on investigation and support. This underlines the fact that the conflict is not between science and Christianity but between world views. Freud's presuppositions are ultimately naturalistic and so must be defended on those terms.

We will make two comments about the claim that Christians project their desires onto God. First, if it is true that God is the Creator and that there is therefore an analogy between him and his work, it is not surprising that there are resemblances between the human and the divine Father. In fact, Freud may have discovered one of the mechanisms that God uses for creating the idea of himself in the human mind. From the experience of a human father we gain some limited perception of a heavenly Father. John Hick comments:

> If the relation of a human father to his children is, as the Judaic-Christian tradition teaches, analogous to God's relationship to man, it is not surprising that human beings should think of God as their heavenly Father and should come to know him through the infant's experience of utter dependence and the growing child's experience of being loved, cared for and disciplined within a family. (1973a, p. 36)

Although human fatherhood may reflect the divine Father, a word of caution is in order. Scripture reminds us that the real source of our idea of fatherhood is God, not our earthly father. As Paul says, "I fall on my knees before the Father (from whom all fatherhood, earthly or heavenly, derives its name)" (Eph 3:14-15 Phillips).

Second, it is understandable that people would invest their religious heroes with characteristics like themselves. But Christianity claims that what is most important about God is that he is unlike us. He is not only loving Father and protecting Mother, but also pure Judge and holy Savior. How could such exalted

conceptions come from creatures ruled by dark instincts?
B. F. Skinner. If Freud is considered by many to be out of date,
B. F. Skinner continues to exert strong influence within faculties
of psychology. Skinner and his many disciples present religion as
a product of positive reinforcement. Skinner is the most recent
exponent of a long tradition usually associated with materialism
whose most famous expression is twentieth-century pragmatism.
Rejecting all idealistic interpretations of behavior, most pragma-
tists insisted that knowledge is a matter of muscle and reflex.
Speaking about thinking, pragmatist John Dewey once remarked:
   Habits formed in the process of exercising biological aptitudes
   are the sole agents of observation, recollection, foresight and
   judgment: a mind or consciousness or soul in general which
   performs these operations is a myth. . . . Knowledge which is
   not projected against the black unknown lives in the muscles
   not in the consciousness. (vol. 3, p. i)
Personality is nothing more than a neurophysiological mechanism that can be manipulated and trained. On this assumption
John F. Watson launched his famous school of psychology, *behaviorism,* with a series of lectures at Columbia University in 1912.
His starting point was that "man is an animal different from other
animals only in the types of behavior he displays" (p. v). Those
who speak of the soul as something separate from the body are
using empty terms "uncritically as a part of [their] social and
literary traditions" (p. 10). The goal of research is to predict and
control human behavior. Watson's description of love is an example of where behaviorism can lead: "The stimulus to love response apparently is stroking of the skin, tickling, gentle rocking
or patting. The responses are especially easy to bring out (in a
child) by the stimulation of what, for lack of a better term, we
may call the erogenous zones" (p. 155). This is what is left of behavior unique to the person.
   In 1971 behaviorist views captured the popular imagination
with the publication of B. F. Skinner's book *Beyond Freedom and
Dignity.* Skinner's thesis is that everything in human behavior can
be accounted for by environmental conditioning. There is no

"ego" unlinked to stimulus and response. What we call the self is "a repertoire of behavior appropriate to a given set of contingencies" (p. 199). The idea of some essential "human nature," some enduring self, blinds us to the real causes of behavior. We must abolish such conceptions. All our actions are explained by the mechanism Skinner calls *operant conditioning:* "When a bit of behavior is followed by a certain consequence, it is more likely to occur again, and a consequence having this effect is called a reinforcer" (p. 27). In place of Freud's *instinct,* read *habit.* When we claim an action is "free," we simply do not see its real causes.

Let us see how behaviorism understands the main themes of Christianity. What we call sin is merely habit deriving from a history of reinforcement. God is introduced as an explanatory fiction. Heaven and hell are the final positive and negative reinforcements, effective through their constant invocation in human behavior. The person is more than a dog, but like a dog he is within the range of scientific analysis.

One might well wonder if there is anything of intrinsic value for Skinner. Survival is "the only value according to which a culture is eventually to be judged, and any practice that furthers survival has survival value by definition" (p. 136). But this limited faith does not keep Skinner from erecting an exalted vision for the future.

It is hard to imagine a world in which people live together without quarreling, maintain themselves by producing the food, shelter, and clothing they need, enjoy themselves and contribute to the enjoyment of others in art, music, literature and games, consume only a reasonable part of the resources of the world and add as little as possible to its pollution, bear no more children than can be raised decently, continue to explore the world around them and discover better ways of dealing with it, and come to know themselves accurately and, therefore, manage themselves effectively. Yet all this is possible, and even the slightest sign of progress should bring a kind of change which would correct the impression that "we neither can nor need to do anything for ourselves," and promote a

"sense of freedom and dignity" by building "a sense of confidence and worth." In other words, it should abundantly reinforce those who have been induced by their culture to work for its survival. . . . We have not yet seen what man can make of man. (pp. 214-15)
One wonders if a Christian vision of hope and humanity "reinforced" this utopian dream; positive reinforcement for it is not to be found in our daily newspaper or in the common experience of mankind.

How should we respond to this serious attack on Christianity? First we must recognize that chemical, physiological and environmental processes do influence human behavior. This no one wishes to deny. But that they are the ultimate determinative factors is difficult to support. Scientists debate among themselves the role of heredity and environment. How do we account for variation in the behavior of twins raised in the same environment? At stake here is the view of the person as a responsible agent responding to and creatively informing his or her environment. Granted that many factors influence and limit our behavior, are we not still able and responsible to make what we can of what we have been given? Human ability to choose is graphically portrayed in the New Testament parable of the talents (Mt 25:14-30).

In fact it seems impossible to live without choosing and pursuing values. Skinner has claimed that the survival of the race is the only final value. But how can he rise above his environment and make this assertion? Skinner responds that any culture not valuing survival will simply cease to exist. As he put it, "So much the worse for that culture" (p. 137). Who says that is not "so much the better"?

It becomes obvious from reading Skinner that he holds a whole range of primarily humanistic values that presumably result from his own conditioning. Now his methodology can tell us why he values certain things (the descriptive function), but it cannot tell us which things he should value (the prescriptive function). Why are his values any more valid than, say, the value of the survival of the Aryan race in Fascist Germany?

All these considerations become especially crucial and omi-
nous when the question of directing the future of humanity
comes up. Skinner sees social planning as an exciting way to elim-
nate all of society's defects. But who, we might ask, will locate
these defects and control the direction of our evolution? Skinner
implies that this does not matter since the conditioners are themselves conditioned. Stephen Evans comments:

> Surely the slightest historical knowledge or reflection on the
> contemporary worldwide political scene makes it abundantly
> clear that it makes an enormous difference who the "control-
> lers" of a society may be. . . . With this god-like knowledge,
> they now possess the ability to change those conditions and
> presumably their own values as well. But in what directions
> should the changes be made? No good answer seems to be
> forthcoming. (pp. 55-56)

What Skinner never does is argue for the truth of his views over
against other perspectives. In the past, Skinner seems to be saying, people were afflicted with a false consciousness: but now our
perspective of things is correct. Their views resulted from reinforced habit, but this is the final truth. And what of the assertion
that all behavior results from environmental conditioning? What
scientific experiment could ever prove this? One can of course
prove that this or that behavior is conditioned, but that there is
no unconditioned act cannot possibly be proven. It seems after
all that this view is a philosophical theory about the nature of the
world masquerading in scientific dress.

One point made against Freud is valid here also: the causal
origin of my belief is logically separate from its truth or falsity.
I may have been conditioned to believe certain things are true,
and these things may after all be true. Even if modern people
(whoever they are) cannot conceive of God because of unfortu-
nate conditioning (like Skinner's, for example), God may go right
on existing.

Skinner's own background may in fact account for his beliefs.
In that case they may not be valid for someone who is the product
of different conditioning. In the August 1971 issue of *Psychology*

Today, T. George Harris says of Skinner's upbringing:
His family was warm and stable, and much concerned about good behavior. "I was taught to fear God, the police and what people will think," he recalls, and he suspects his reaction may have led him to try proving that people don't think at all. An old-maid school teacher taught him English composition in the public school and Old Testament language and morals in the Presbyterian Sunday School. His father took him through the country jail to show him the punishment he would face if he were to develop à criminal mind. He was never whipped. Once when he used a bad word, his mother washed out his mouth with soap. Grandmother Skinner had him peer into the glowing coals of the parlor stove to gain a sense of hell. (p. 34)
This ad hominem argument does not of course prove Skinner's views false, but it does suggest that given other experiences, his views might have differed. How then are we to trust his views?

Freud himself points out the difficulties of building a behaviorist utopia:
It may be doubted whether it is possible at all, or at any rate as yet, at the present stage of our control over nature, to set up cultural regulations of this kind. It may be asked where the number of superior, unswerving, and disinterested leaders are to come from who are to act as educators of the future generations, and it may be alarming to think of the enormous amount of coercion that will inevitably be required before these intentions can be carried out. (p. 7)
The social sciences, like the empirical, simply cannot operate outside some larger framework. We can condition behavior, but toward what end? The empirical and the descriptive call for (and often spill into) the normative and the prescriptive. Science demands a comprehensive commitment. We insist that it is within the Christian framework that scientific insights are best used. The biblical system of values can best give direction to human development.

One further point calls for comment in this connection. The ever-present danger of the social sciences is reductionism. If we observe wish fulfillment in our thinking, we conclude that it accounts for all religion; if we see the influence of conditioning on our behavior, we conclude that no behavior can be "free." But we need not make these conclusions, and in fact many scientists refuse to do so. We will see even more clearly in our discussion of sociology that valid insight only becomes dangerous when it is made into a universal principle.

Sociology

If psychology studies the behavior of individuals, sociology focuses on collective behavior and the structures and institutions expressing and shaping that behavior. While psychologists may attribute religious faith to influences upon the individual, sociologists see religion as a product of social forces supported by what they call *plausibility structures*. Beliefs, in this view, are developed in a broad conversation among members of a culture and continue to be credible as long as they receive social support. The challenge to Christianity is only too obvious: the world view that Christians consider "absolute truth" is actually a function of the social context that produces and reinforces it.

The father of this perspective on religion was Emile Durkheim, who in 1915 published his classic study on *The Elementary Forms of the Religions Life*. Durkheim's basic insight was that people live under the laws of a particular society which molds and shapes them even when they are not aware of it. The sociologist seeks to account for human behavior by discovering the inner dynamic of a social structure; this frequently means disregarding motives that people claim for their actions. Durkheim's point is not that social forces determine belief, but that religion is nothing more than the mythological expression of such forces and the means by which individuals come to terms with them. The final reference in religion is not God (or gods) but society. Durkheim says: "We have seen that this reality, which mythologies have represented under so many different forms, but which is the universal and eternal objective cause of these [religious] sensations sui generis out of which religious experience is made, is society" (p. 465).

Religion is simply the concentrated form and expression of the collective life.

Durkheim's study has led to several assumptions used by sociologists of religion to understand religious behavior. The first is that society determines human behavior and thus forms religious beliefs. Peter Berger explains this view as follows:

Most of the time the game has been "fixed" long before we arrive on the scene. All that is left for us to do, most of the time, is to play it with more or less enthusiasm. The professor stepping in front of his class, the judge pronouncing sentence, the preacher badgering his congregation, the commander ordering his troops into battle—all these are engaged in actions that have been predefined within very narrow limits. And impressive systems of controls and sanctions stand guard over these limits. (1963, p. 87)

Our supposedly freely chosen lifestyle is really a "game" or "role" fixed by society. Even making a religious commitment, what Christians call conversion, is only exchanging one role and the expectations that go with it for another defined by a different identity group. If we could exhaustively explore all the factors at work, we could completely explain people's behavior and beliefs. There would be no surprises; it is all in the cards.

This leads to a second assumption, called *functionalism*. However else individuals perceive them, social institutions can be explained by their functions in society, which account for their origin and justify their continued existence. Following Durkheim. sociologists have studied the role of religious symbols and rites in maintaining social integration and cohesion. A functionalist might explain religion as follows. Human existence is a perpetual quest for a meaningful structure in which to understand experience, a structure that will provide shelter in extreme (what sociologists call *marginal*) situations. Symbols and rituals provide assurance that the world has not gone out of control. Doctrines such as immortality and heaven, rites such as novenas and prayers for the sick are useful in marginal situations. They provide what Berger calls a "sacred Cosmos" in which the individual is sheltered from threatening forces (see 1969a). Such protective beliefs are essential to the maintenance of social order. Here again we meet Freud's conception of religion as wish fulfillment, but this time it is understood as a social rather than an individual mechanism.

A third assumption, growing out of social determinism and functionalism, has been called *voluntarism*. Some sociologists of religion, notably Karl Marx and Max Weber, have studied the motives or drives of social groups and the operation of these drives over a period of time. These motives are often not claimed by the groups themselves; indeed most often they operate unconsciously. Marx used the term *ideology* to explain the motive of religion in a given society. Religion, Marx believed, sanctions human alienation from the world. It justifies and perpetuates economic conditions which, according to Marx, oppress the worker. It provides hope in another world to compensate for the lack of hope in this. Ideology is used especially by the ruling classes to rationalize social behavior. When a society's economic conditions are corrected, religion will disappear, since the need for rationalization will be gone. As we will see later, religion's main function, according to Marx, is to maintain the status quo within a social structure.

Max Weber also analyzed the motive force of religion. In his famous study of Protestantism and capitalism, he claimed that an identifiable complex of factors (which he called an *ethos*) in Protestantism motivated the development of capitalism. He defined this ethos as "a certain methodical, rational way of life which—given certain conditions—paved the way for the 'spirit' of modern capitalism. The premiums were placed upon 'proving' oneself before God in the sense of attaining salvation . . . and 'proving' oneself before men in the sense of socially holding one's own" (p. 321). Weber's thesis has provoked much controversy. Some have accused him of dogmatism and of failing to allow for other modernizing factors. But his way of dealing with religious belief is all too common: he viewed religion in terms of its function in society and not as ideas which are either true or false.

How can Christians respond to sociologists' way of handling religious faith? We often dismiss this approach because it seems to reduce religion to a prop in society. Our reaction is understandable: more than one university student has lost interest in Christianity when he or she learned to understand it in terms of social dynamics. But we must recognize that, within the limits of its own descriptive method, the sociological approach to religion is valid. Berger points out that sociology, by describing the social conditions of our knowledge and belief, can liberate us from the tyranny of the present. Modern theologians may teach that the Christian message must be removed from outdated frameworks and expressed in ways understandable by "modern man." Such an approach implies that whereas past pictures of the world were false, ours is the final truth. Berger calls such a view "sociologically naive." What is good for the goose is good for the gander. The present picture of the world results just as much from social and historical forces as any past picture. Sociology may help us understand how a modern person's mind is formed by a constant media barrage—as Berger notes, "We may understand and sympathize with his predicament, [but] there is no reason whatever to stand in awe of it" (1969b, p. 56). In other words, we may understand perfectly why modern consciousness cannot conceive of God, without being compelled to conclude that God therefore does not exist. The defect, as Berger points out, may lie rather in modern consciousness than in the religious tradition (1969a, Appendix 1). God's existence does not depend on human conceptual ability. The function of a religion does not determine its truth or falsity.

Moreover, sociology helps us understand how society functions and why religion is losing (or gaining) ground. Much useful study has been done on secularization in Western societies. British sociologist Bryan Wilson, for example, has argued that the progressive rationalization of the social structure—the encroachment of institutions over the individual—has threatened the survival of nonnatural explanations. Studies like this which describe the influence of social forces on belief are valuable to Christians who wish to proclaim the gospel intelligibly.

But it is a chastened sociology that Christians will appreciate, one that recognizes the limitations of the functional view of religion. Society's role in shaping religious faith may be freely admitted without reducing religion to a projection of society's structure. H. H. Farmer points out that Durkheim fails to account for the universal reach of Christian convictions. Society may influence me to love my tribe or race, but how can it impress upon me the view that God loves all people and that each person is obligated to love everyone he or she encounters? Neither can Durkheim account for Christianity's prophetic conscience. Can social structure explain Jeremiah or John the Baptist? Durkheim's view may describe a closed, static society, but how does it account for ethical innovation and change? (See Hick, 1973a, pp. 33-34.) An entirely naturalistic interpretation of Christianity has a hard time explaining signs of supernatural direction.

We return to our recurrent theme that one must recognize the limitations of partial perspectives. While religion obviously has a variety of social functions, it does not follow that religion is nothing but its social function. You may bring a small vessel to a fountain, but do not blame the fountain if your cup can hold only a little. You may choose to examine Christianity as behavior or as a function in society, but do not then blame Christianity if that is all you see in it. To be adequately interpreted, the findings of social science must be put into a larger perspective.

Remember that limitation is inherent in the scientific method. Empirical science must operate within the assumption of universal causality; every effect must be assumed to have an antecedent cause or condition (Berger, 1963, p. 122). Within its limits the scientific picture is valid; the world in general does operate as a system of cause and effect. But this is not the whole story, and not all scientists today argue that it is. The scientific method alone cannot account for any effect that is its own cause. The scientific framework, when taken alone, excludes not only God's intervention but also human freedom, for these by definition have no anterior cause. To account for these factors one must introduce another frame of reference that allows for the reality of the personal.

But not all sociological theory is a threat to Christianity. Some sociologists recognize that the person can be understood not only in terms of function in society but also in terms of ability to act counter to society's dictates. A person can transcend his or her situation and pursue individual values and goals. Sociologists call this dimension of human behavior "intentionality," "role distance" or "charisma." Although it is foolish to deny the pervasive and inescapable influence of our culture, this influence does not prevent people from acting on their environment and working to change existing structures. If this were not possible, there would be no hope for bettering the human condition, and all development would be impossible.

From a Christian point of view, human agency is particularly important, for Christians believe that the person is ultimately responsible to a personal God who transcends the world and yet works out his purpose within it. Indeed for Christianity the absolute element in religion is not the conceptions or symbols that guide behavior, but the existence of this personal God. The person, whatever his or her situation, is responsible to obey God and to reflect his character. And while a person's psychological and social situation must provide the context for his or her actions, this situation is always capable of being transformed into a vehicle that more clearly reflects God's character. Christianity calls this process redemption, and there is ample evidence for it both in the biblical record and in the lives of many Christians.

That a particular social and psychological situation can reflect God's goodness is perfectly consistent with the Christian view of creation. For as Peter Berger observes, "If the religious projections of man correspond to a reality that is superhuman and supernatural, then it seems logical to look for traces of this reality in the projector himself" (1969b, p. 59). In contrast to Durkheim, we must insist that the final reference point is God's character and not society. It is not God who reflects society, but rather society which is destined one day to reflect God.

Questions for Review

1. Give two reasons why the social sciences and Christianity should not conflict.
2. What is Freud's view of the nature of religion?
3. How do you respond to the charge that Christianity is nothing but wish fulfillment?
4. Discuss the charge that God is a projection of the primal father.
5. How does a behaviorist explain religion?
6. Respond to Skinner from a Christian point of view.
7. How does Durkheim see the relation between society and religion?
8. What is the functionalist view of religion?
9. What are the positive functions of sociological method for the Christian?
10. Name some objections to Durkheim's view of religion.
11. What is the Christian view of the person in society?

CHAPTER NINE

The Problem of Evil

I t is hard to imagine anyone who has not at one time or another been perplexed by the problem of evil. If God is loving and good and also all-powerful, how can he let his creatures suffer as they do? This difficulty has troubled many people throughout the history of Christianity, and although many solutions have been offered, much discussion of the problem continues today. While we cannot expect to solve the problem within the scope of this brief discussion, we may show the directions a solution might take. We should realize that we consider here a problem which has eluded thinkers for thousands of years, one of the mysteries of human existence, a mystery bound up in the closest way with religious experience. We ought not to approach this problem casually. "It is in suffering," Jürgen Mottmann has argued, "that the whole human question about God arises." For suffering is not merely an academic question but the "open wound of life in this world" (pp. 47, 49).

On one level it is necessary only to show that the existence of evil does not constitute an insuperable obstacle to faith in God and Christianity. To do this one has only to show that there is no formal or informal inconsistency to the existence of evil and belief in God. But on the principle that a good offense is the best defense, many Christians have gone on to suggest why God has allowed evil. They have offered what is called a *theodicy*, or a justification for God's permitting evil. Our approach will combine these approaches. We will define the problem, look at several non-Christian approaches and finally suggest five directions from which a Christian may approach the problem. While no single argument may prove incontrovertible, a cumulative case may be made for the goodness of God in the face of the existence of evil. (See the diagram on p. 165, where these arguments are related to one another.)

The Problem Stated

Even before the coming of Christ, Greek philosophers had formulated the problem of evil. Epicurus (341-270 B.C.), quoted by Lactantius (A.D. 260-340), put it like this:

God either wishes to take away evils, and is unable; or he is able and unwilling; or he is neither willing nor able, or he is both willing and able. If he is willing and is unable, he is feeble, which is not in accordance with the character of God; if he is able and unwilling, he is envious, which is equally at variance with God; if he is neither willing nor able he is both envious and feeble, and therefore not God; if he is both willing and able, which alone is suitable to God, from what source then are evils? or why does he not remove them?

Thomas Aquinas, the great medieval theologian, recognized in this dilemma of Epicurus one of the chief obstacles to Christianity. He sought to understand the problem by distinguishing primary from secondary causes. Though God is obviously the primary cause of all that exists, evil is to be attributed to secondary causes for which God is not morally responsible. "For because we have proven that every agent acts insofar as it acts through God's power, with God being thus the cause of all effects and acts, and since we proved that evil and defects in beings directed by divine providence come from the condition of the secondary causes, which themselves may be defective, it is obvious that evil actions, understood as defective, do not originate from God but from their defective proximate causes" (*Compendium of Theology,* chap. 141).

In modern thought the problem has been given renewed prominence by David Hume, who argued that we cannot know any cause except by its effects. Therefore, in order to argue for divine goodness on the basis of natural theology, it would be necessary to deny absolutely the misery and wickedness of man (*Dialogues Concerning Natural Religion,* chap. 10). If you wish to believe in divine goodness, Hume concluded, you may do so by faith, but you certainly cannot draw this conclusion by observing the world.

There are many sorts of evil, both natural and moral, in the world. Some sorts, such as earthquakes and hurricanes, seem necessary to the created structure. Others relate more directly to human failure and perversity. We are coming to understand, however, that these evils may be more interrelated than we had previously imagined. Weather conditions may not be completely unrelated to human greed and selfishness (what long-term effect, for example, will result from a substantial reduction of the Amazonian jungles in Brazil?). Sickness may be more a result of improper lifestyle and diet than a blow of fate. But why did God allow a world in which such horrible eventualities exist? Since he is all-powerful and all-good, could he not have conceived of an all-good world where evil was absent?

From this brief look at the way this problem has been formulated, we clearly see that the difficulty stems from the idea of one God who is all-powerful and good. Believers in many gods or in a finite God do not have such a problem. Those who believe in no god, however, while they may have no problem of evil to face, have a different problem on their hands. We could call it "the problem of good." What is the meaning of goodness if there is no standard by which to measure it? They may try to escape this dilemma by insisting that the world is a complex natural fact in which goodness and evil appear by chance. It is the Christian who claims that the world ought to be other than it is and so is faced with the challenge of accounting for the evil that exists. Interestingly, many people who do not believe in God seem to bear a great resentment against Christians and against God for a problem which on their own assumptions does not exist at all. As E. L. Mascall comments wryly, "This is very mysterious, and almost leads one to suspect that the atheists have been indulging in a little surreptitious theism on the quiet" (1966, p. 183).

Since this problem is unique to orthodox Christianity, we may dismiss unorthodox solutions to the problem. The seventeenth-century philosopher Spinoza, for example, believed that everything follows by logical necessity from the divine essence. All that exists, both good and evil, is a necessary expression of the fullness of divine creativity. Others have taken the view that evil is only an illusion resulting from a faulty perspective. Eastern philosophy suggests this point of view, and in the West Mary Baker Eddy has followed a similar line: "Nothing is real and eternal, nothing is Spirit, but God and his idea. Evil has no reality. It is neither person, place nor thing, but simply a belief, an illusion of material sense" (p. 71). Dualists account for evil by positing two eternal forces struggling for supremacy. Manichaeism and Zoroastrianism both maintained that there are two basic principles of reality, one good and one evil. A variation of this approach is to assume that God is not all-powerful but is, like us, finite. So God himself is struggling against the evil reality and we are invited to join in his battle. But these solutions evade the problem by redefining the terms and are thus unacceptable to Christians.

Christianity has refused to avoid the problem by suggesting that evil is unreal or unimportant. It is precisely because evil is so pervasive that the problem of evil is so acute. While there is no level of created reality that is frowned upon as such (see 1 Tim

4:3-4), in the biblical view evil and depravity have penetrated to all of reality as we know it. Nevertheless, Christians insist, God remains just and righteous in his purposes even if he is the creator and sustainer of this present evil world. It is a Christian conviction then that evil is permitted by a sovereign God in some way that is ultimately compatible with his goodness. How can we argue for this?

The Christian Response

Appeal to origins. A moment's thought makes clear that this is not a single problem but a set of interrelated questions. One aspect of the problem of evil is the question of origin. How did evil happen in a world that was created good? Of course even if we answer this question we will not explain the presence of evil; describing *how* a person came to your house is not the same thing as understanding *why* he came. But understanding the origin of evil may help us understand the abnormality of the present situation.

Augustine took this approach in his famous work *City of God.* God, he noted, who is ultimate goodness, created a world that was essentially good. Evil resulted when the finite will turned from desire for the highest good to desire for some lesser good. "Even the nature of the Devil, in so far as it is a nature, is not evil; it was perversity—not being true to itself—that made it bad. The Devil did not 'stand in the truth,' and therefore, did not escape the judgment of truth" (XIX, p. 13). Two implications of this view have been much discussed in the history of Christianity. The first, Augustine's view, is that evil does not belong to the essence of the created order but to its present fallen existence. As subsequent philosophers formulated it, evil is a privation (or negation) of the good creation, and not something positive; it is accidental, not essential. As one modern commentator has said, this approach seeks to give an historical rather than an ontological account of the origin of evil. That is, human and natural existence as it was created, both in the whole process and in the individual creature, was good. Evil is not to be accounted for by the nature of this order; it results from the wrong choices of moral beings. Evil is something that *happened* in the course of the exercise of freedom (Gilkey, p. 218). All evil that now exists therefore can be accounted for by the wrong choices of free moral agents. But if this tells us *how* evil came about, it does not help us see *why*. For this we must carry our inquiry a step further.

Appeal to mystery. The Christian may respond to this challenge by appealing to either the creaturely limitation of human understanding or the mystery inherent in freedom. In the first instance the Christian may have to say quite simply: though I believe God has a reason for permitting evil, I do not know what it is. This response may not be as strange as it first seems. There are many events in life that puzzle us but that we accept as capable of explanation. Every time we visit a physician we show our trust in explanations that we do not understand. On this assumption Christians' inability to explain evil may tell us more about Christians than about God. Alvin Plantinga says of this inability: "Why suppose that if God *does* have a good reason for permitting evil, the theist would be the first to know? Perhaps God has a good reason, but that reason is too complicated for us to understand" (p. 10). So our inability to explain the presence of evil may give us insight into the limitation of our thinking about God, but may not in itself offer an obstacle to the rationality of religious faith.

But the heart of the appeal to mystery lies in what is sometimes called the *free will defense*. That is, evil can be accounted for by the fact that God made morally free agents capable of making wrong moral choices. Although nothing possible lies beyond God's power, what is not logically possible is also impossible for God. God cannot do the logically impossible because there is nothing there for him to do, only "a meaningless conjunction of words" (Hick, 1973a, p. 39). A free agent that could do no evil is such a logical impossibility. Now God could have avoided the evils we experience by not creating a world at all, but this hardly solves our problem. Given the fact that God did create, it is at least possible that God could not logically create a world containing moral good but no moral evil. A moment's reflection will show why this is so. If George is actually free with regard to a given moral act, then it is up to George whether or not to perform that act; it is not up to God. True, God could have created a world in which people always chose what is right, but it would be difficult to argue that moral freedom existed in such a world. Of course we may see certain influences, such as God's direction, on a person's choice without thereby saying that the choice is not free. We can often predict what our friends will do in a given situation; it does not follow that their actions are not free.

Freedom by definition cannot be reduced to various natural influences, and this makes it impossible to find a rational explanation for the existence of wrong choices. We can point to various influences; we cannot call any of them decisive without denying the possibility of freedom altogether. As Gilkey puts this point, "To find a rational explanation for evil would be to find a natural cause for it. . . . If then sin is not externally determined, ipso facto no reason can be given for it" (p. 220).

It is often asserted that the existence of evil is incompatible with the existence of a good God. In response to this the free will defense suggests that it may not be (logically) within God's power to create a world containing moral good but no moral evil. If this is allowed, no insuperable objection to God's existence can be raised from this quarter (see Plantinga, pp. 45-50).

Appeal to God's larger purposes. One of the strongest defenses against the challenge of evil is based on God's possible purposes in allowing evil. God could be justified in creating a world in which evil is possible if he could achieve a greater good in such a world than in a world where evil is impossible. Now the problem of evil is often posed against the background of a humanistic philosophy. If the ultimate good consists in human pleasure and self-fulfillment (or any other anthropocentric good) and God's purposes must be made to serve these ends, it is hard to see how any answer to the problem of evil could appeal to God's "higher" purposes. But if the supreme end of creation involves transcendent goals, then this approach may prove helpful.

If solution is to be found in the larger purposes of God, however, some indications of this should be evident in the course of God's dealings with his people. Are there such indications? Even a brief glance at Scripture shows that there are. From one point of view the treatment of Joseph by his brothers was a tragedy, and yet in the end Joseph was able to say to his brothers: "As for you, you meant evil against me; but God meant it for good, to bring it about that many people should be kept alive" (Gen 50:20). The book of Job certainly does not picture a world in which evil and human anguish are overlooked; indeed Job struggles manfully against his calamities. Yet God's purposes can be seen in the deepening of Job's faith ("I had heard of thee by the hearing of the ear, but now my eye sees thee" [Job 42:5]) and in the display of God's power to Job, his friends and his family. Lamentations can picture poignant sorrow over the death of a nation and a culture and still see that God's mercies never come to an end (4:22). In the midst of severe national crisis the prophet Isaiah can speak for God: "When you pass through the waters I will be with you; and through the rivers, they will not overwhelm you; when you walk through fire you shall not be burned, and the flame shall not consume you. For I am the LORD your God" (43:2-3). For the Hebrew, unlike the Greek, there could be no ultimate tragedy. He knew that God's purposes would triumph. Suffering was not an inevitable fact on the road to knowledge (as it was for the Greek); it was a reflection of a fallen order and a judgment for sin, yet it was potentially capable of atoning for the guilt of the people (see Isaiah 53).

In the New Testament, God's triumph over evil is clearly presented. From one point of view Christ's death was a great human tragedy, but from the perspective of God's purposes it was a great triumph of God's grace. For in and through the suffering of Christ, the New Testament makes clear, God's victory over sin and death (and ultimately over suffering) is realized. Christ could say to his disciples that they would surely have tribulations in the world, "but be of good cheer, for I have overcome the world" (Jn 16:33). While we cannot develop completely a theory (or theories) of atonement, we can point out that the death of Christ attacked evil on two fronts. First, it dealt with the origin of evil by ransoming the sinner through paying the price for sin. Second, Christ's death and resurrection provided for the renewal of the fallen order (2 Cor 5:21 and Rom 8:19-21). Both ways of dealing with evil follow consistently from the view that evil is privation and not something positive in creation. Since finitude is essentially good, it is possible to have a new creation (2 Cor 5:17) which is a fulfillment of human values and not their negation. Salvation thus is both pardon for wrong done and renewal of the fallen order.

The church is to be the community that exhibits the goodness and perfection of the original creation. Interestingly, it is to be "made perfect through suffering." The death of Christ has put our understanding of evil in a new light. What we call evil has in the providence of God been made into an instrument for the realization of his purposes. While not losing a whit of their bite and intensity, our sufferings have become—potentially at least— tokens of a greater good that God has in store for his people (see Rom 8:18).

Appeal to God's present purposes. We turn to a further argument for the fact that, as Augustine put it, "God judged it better to bring good out of evil than to suffer no evil to exist." On the basis of how God has dealt with evil in the past, and because of his mighty redemptive work, we can perhaps now see how suffering and evil can function in a constructive way in people's lives. That is, the existence of just this world (or one much like it) is necessary to the realization of human character and value.

This view was first presented by Irenaeus (A.D. 130-202). Man is created in the image of God and is capable of realizing this likeness by the pouring out of the Holy Spirit. This life then is understood as the context for gradual spiritual growth—a "vale of soul-making." In the contrasting (and often painful) experience of good and evil a person is taught to love one and despise the other. Thus Adam's sin was more an understandable lapse than a great catastrophe, for man was not so much created perfect as created for perfection. His perfecting lies in the future.

This view, sometimes called the teleological view of evil, has been especially popular in Eastern Orthodox Christianity. Evil is a pedagogic tool to lead people to maturity. Seen in this light, the Fall has a positive significance. As Nicholas Berdyaev put it: "The fall of the first man, Adam, had positive meaning and justification, as a moment in the revelation of creativity, preparing for the appearance of absolute man [Christ]" (pp. 177-78).

One does not have to agree with all the theological implications of Irenaeus's view to see it as a promising line of approach. Granted the presence and pervasiveness of evil, can God use it to accomplish his purpose in people's lives? In natural disasters and times of war we see examples of exceptional bravery, people pulling together to help the suffering in a way inconceivable during normal times. Frequently experiences of hardship produce character and discipline in individual lives.

It might be helpful to imagine for a moment a world in which evil and suffering are absent. Suppose that it were impossible for anyone to injure another; a child could fall from a tree without injury; fraud and deceit would somehow have positive effects on society. It is not hard to see that in such a world there would be no need to work if one was not so inclined; there would be no call to help people in need since there would be no needs. In short, right and wrong would have no meaning, and even creativity and science would be impossible since the world would have no structure to discover or imagine. As John Hick remarks: "Such a world, however well it might promote pleasure, would be very ill adapted for the development of the moral qualities of human personality. In relation to this purpose it might be the worst of all possible worlds!" (Hick, 1973a, pp. 42-43). But one cannot have a moral world without the specter of the harmful effects of immorality. If there is structure and meaning, there must also be the possibility of injury and deceit. That is what it means to live in a moral order.

This becomes clearer when one understands the nature of the Christian life. In the writings of Peter, suffering purifies the church. Paul pictures it as equipping the people of God for ministry. It is a Christian conviction that evil can be used in a higher purpose, that suffering produces saintliness. If this is true, then it is possible that God's unwillingness to create a world in which evil is impossible reflects neither on his goodness nor on his power, but flows from his eternal and unchanging purposes. The relation of suffering to sainthood suggests, says H. W. Robinson, that it is possible to imagine "the relation of the holy grace of the divine Spirit to the guilt of human spirit, and the vision of a world redeemed from its guilt as well as from the power of its sin, in such a way of spiritual transformation that the final result is nobler and richer than a sinless world could ever have been" (p. 74).

Appeal to God's final purposes. Robinson's idea brings us naturally to the final step of inquiring into God's final purposes: our sinful world is "nobler and richer" in what way, and for whom? Part of our problem with evil may lie in our limited knowledge and perspective; we have noted this above and we need to re-emphasize it here. As Mascall notes, any exertion for a goal may involve pain: the athlete running a race, the author trying to meet the publisher's deadline. Perhaps when we view creation in its totality, we will see evil as a necessary element in the meaning of the whole. This solution, called sometimes the *aesthetic* theme, goes back to Augustine Evil in some way contributes to the complex good that God will bring about. Not sin and misery in themselves, but persons capable of sin and misery, are necessary to perfection. Moreover, God is able to use even the imperfections and perversity of his creatures to reach the final result. As the psalmist confesses: "Surely the wrath of men shall praise thee" (Ps 76:10).

Do we have any evidence that the aesthetic theme is true? I believe it is possible to show from the biblical picture of the new heavens and new earth that God's final purposes will have precisely this result. Now heaven is pictured as the place where God will wipe away every tear from our eyes (Rev 7:17). Moreover the saints that have suffered will be wearing white robes, suggesting that evil and injustice will find their compensation in God's final settlement. But more than this, Revelation pictures God's people praising throughout all eternity the Lamb that was slain, that is, the ransom paid for moral evil. The crucifixion, an obvious result of evil and injustice, will not have been passed over and overcome; it will actually be featured—an object of eternal devotion and wonder.

The context of the final reconciliation also deserves notice, for in the renewed and restored order natural evil will be completely overcome. It will be a perfect environment for the new moral order where, 1 Corinthians 15:28 tells us, God will be all in all. Thus the final purpose of God signifies a perfection and realization of the purposes we glimpse only imperfectly now. In union with Christ, Christians believe, we have a way of dealing with evil, both natural and moral. Just as sin arose in the course of history, so it has been dealt with in the course of that same history; just as moral evil meant the dislocation and perversion of the whole created order, so redemption means the restoration of that very order to its full integrity. F. J. Sheed sums this up well: "Suffering would be altogether intolerable if there were no God, but can be turned to the highest uses of man if there be a God. Atheism answers that the fact of suffering proves that there is no God. But this does not reduce the world's sufferings by one hairbreadth, it only takes away hope" (quoted in Mascall, 1966, p. 184).

Even hope, however, does not provide all the answers to our questions about evil, for there is much here that we simply cannot understand. But consistent with our view of Christianity as God's project, we insist that the problem of evil ultimately must be approached practically rather than theoretically. For what, after all, do our neat answers mean to people who are suffering? In the end we must all face this issue not by philosophical explanations but by living in and through the evils of a fallen world. Only the strength of the God who has come to bear our sufferings in Jesus Christ is adequate to the challenge of human anguish. For Christ has not only endured evil but triumphed over it in the cross and the resurrection, and he allows us to taste this triumph by the gift of the Holy Spirit. So that although sin and death continue to hold sway, for the Christian their hopeless sting is gone (see 1 Cor 15:51-58).

Questions for Review

1. Explain Epicurus's dilemma concerning the problem of evil.
2. Give at least two solutions that Christians cannot accept.
3. How did Augustine believe evil came about? Give two implications of his view.
4. Explain the *free will defense*.
5. Why is it permissible for a Christian to say that he does not know why God allowed evil, but that God knows?
6. Give some examples from Scripture where God used evil to achieve good.
7. Describe Irenaeus's view of the world as a vale of soul-making.
8. How is Christ's death relevant to the problem of evil?
9. Give two ways in which the final purposes of God help us understand evil.

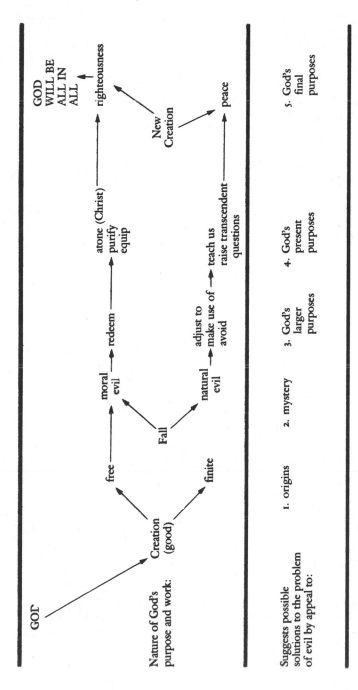

GOD

Nature of God's
purpose and work:

GOD
WILL BE
ALL IN
ALL — righteousness

Creation
(good)

free — moral
evil — redeem — atone (Christ)
purify
equip

New
Creation — peace

Fall

finite

natural
evil — adjust to
make use of — teach us
avoid — raise transcendent
questions

Suggests possible
solutions to the problem
of evil by appeal to:

1. origins

2. mystery

3. God's
larger
purposes

4. God's
present
purposes

5. God's
final
purposes

Approaches to the Problem of Evil

CHAPTER TEN

Marxism

*I*n many parts of the world today the most serious challenges to Christianity come from social and economic pressures rather than from intellectual attack. Arguments often seem remote to people concerned with day-to-day survival. Communism and Marxism, however, claim to offer practical hope to people caught in the hopeless cycle of poverty. In the West the challenge provided by Marxism may seem distant; in many parts of the world it is far from academic. For millions the name Karl Marx is more familiar and more inspiring than the name Jesus Christ. In this chapter we will introduce some of the basic teachings of Marxism, especially as they challenge and provide an alternative to Christianity. Then we will seek to show that any valid Marxist insights either are derived from Christian teaching or are perfectly consistent with Christianity.

The Challenge of Communism

While there have been various forms of communism throughout history, it was Karl Marx (1818-83) who gave communism its modern definition. Marx was raised in a Jewish family which converted to Christianity (perhaps as much for economic as religious reasons) when he was six. At 24 he earned a doctorate in philosophy; the same year he became editor of a left-wing newspaper in Germany. Before long he was forced into exile, first to Paris (where he met Frederick Engels), then in 1849 to London, where he settled and lived in poverty, studying and writing quietly in the British Museum. In 1848 his famous *Communist Manifesto* appeared, and in 1867 his study of economic development was published under the title *Capital*.

For Marx matter is the ultimate reality, and what we call spiritual realities are really the expression of highly organized matter. Laws of matter are the final human environment and these come to their most important expression in economic organization. He wrote: "It is not the consciousness of men that determine their being, but on the contrary, their social being that determines their consciousness." Having espoused the views of the left-wing Hegelians, Marx believed that reality was a natural process of developing economic structures, and that cultural and religious forms simply express these underlying structures.

More important even than his philosophical orientation was the sociological and economic framework Marx developed out of it. His basic premise is that the production and exchange of products is the foundation of every social structure. Engels, writing in 1888, expressed this assumption in these words:

> In every historical epoch, the prevailing mode of economic production and exchange, and the social organization necessarily following from it, form the basis upon which is built up, and from which alone can be explained, the political and intellectual history of that epoch; that consequently the whole history of mankind . . . has been a history of class struggles, contests between exploiting and exploited, ruling and oppressed classes; that the history of these class struggles forms a series of evolu-

tions in which, nowadays a stage has been reached where the exploited and oppressed class—the proletariat—cannot attain its emancipation . . . without at the same time . . . emancipating society at large. (Marx and Engels, preface)
The dynamic interplay of economic forces stimulates development, what we call history. This process follows a natural evolution from primitive communalism to slave-owning economy, to feudalism, to capitalism and finally to the classless society.

Writing against the background of the exploitation and excesses of nineteenth-century industrialization, Marx and Engels analyzed conditions they saw around them and developed their specific steps in historical development. First, they believed that division of labor makes money important and forces the working classes to sell their labor for money in order to live. Power slowly begins to be attached to those who own and control the means of production (capitalists). But this power is bought at an awful price. For on Marxist assumptions, only socially necessary labor (that is, the amount of human labor necessary to produce an object) creates real value; any money obtained through the sale of the product over and above this real value is stolen from the worker. Since the worker derives his personal value from his work and part of this is taken from him, he is said to be *alienated* by his employer. Alienation is a key concept in Marxist thought. It means to Marx, "domination of living men by dead matter," and it results when the labor of the worker is bought and sold.

This grand process called *historical materialism* contains within itself the engine for its movement. Here Marx shows the influence of the philosopher George W. F. Hegel (1770-1831), who taught that history represents the various stages of the developing spirit. Marx replaced Hegel's absolute spirit with economic forms. Each stage creates its own enemies which will overthrow the system and create a new structure. Capitalism alienates the worker and prepares the way for the revolution in which he will seek to regain his "surplus value," for the very conditions of life imposed by capitalism teach the worker to cooperate against his employer. We have reached the stage when the final revolution is in sight, for the dictatorship of the proletariat is the penultimate condition. After this, Marxists believe, the state will wither away and eventually disappear altogether.

For the purposes of our study we should notice that, on Marxist premises, the developing order always creates cultural and religious forms appropriate to it. The forms of society express and at the same time legitimate underlying economic realities. Although most people believe that the ideals and goals of a given group determine the shape of its institutions, according to Communist theory the process works in the opposite direction. The economic reality is basic; ideals and goals are invented later to justify the existing structure. This is the basis of Marx's concept of *ideology*, a term he often uses in a derogatory way. A society's ideology is a collective illusion giving social support to the economic conditions holding sway. All social institutions including religion can be understood as expressions of ideology.

The Marxist Critique of Religion

To understand Marx's views of religion, we must say something about philosopher Ludwig Feuerbach (1804-72). In his famous book *The Essence of Christianity* (1840), Feuerbach called religion "the dream of the human spirit." Religious ideas are merely the projection of people's dreams onto an illusionary object. People create the objects of their dreams. The Incarnation, for example, is nothing but the reflection of the human dream to become God. Obviously, then, religious faith tells us more about people than it does about the supposed object of faith.

Feuerbach's views served as a starting point for Marx's critique of religion. Marx proceeded to ask: In what circumstance do people project their ideal powers on superhuman forces? What are the social causes of this phenomenon? This was far more interesting to Marx than the philosophical speculations of Feuerbach. As he put it in his seventh thesis on Feuerbach: "Feuerbach does not see that the 'religious sentiment' is itself a social product, and that the abstract individual whom he analyses belongs to a particular form of society" (Marx, 1963, p. 84).

Religion then is part of a society's ideology. In Marx's famous expression, it is the "opium of the people." By this Marx meant that religion buttresses the economic status quo; the parson and the landlord go hand in hand. Because of the promises held out by religion, people remain contented with the vile condition in which they find themselves. In Marx's words:

Religious distress is at the same time the *expression* of real distress and the *protest* against real distress. Religion is the sigh of the oppressed creature, the heart of a heartless world just as it is the spirit of a spiritless situation. It is the *opium* of the people. (Quoted in Aptheker, pp. 5-6)

Remember the phenomenon of religion necessarily reflects a people's social conditions. What is wrong is not religion itself, but the social conditions that give rise to religious illusions. Marx continues:

The abolition of religion as the *illusory* happiness of the people is required for their real happiness. The demand to give up the illusions about its condition is the demand to give up a condition which *needs illusions*. The criticism of religion is therefore *in embryo the criticism of the vale of woe*, the *halo* of which is religion. (Ibid., Marx's italics)

Although Marx and Lenin insisted that party members actively oppose religion, they claimed that this opposition was educational in nature. After all, the people cannot be blamed for illusions arising from social conditions. Since, on Marxist assumptions, religion will die a natural death, the state in principle may be tolerant of faith. In some cases, however, the Communist state has thought it necessary to attack religion because of its supposed alliance with capitalist or oppressive forces. In other situations, such as in Poland or Latin America, overt opposition to religion has by necessity been given up altogether.

Whether the Marxist critique of Christianity is essential to Marxism as a method of sociological analysis has been the subject of much debate. Some Christians in Latin America have believed it possible to separate Marxist social analysis from its philosophical underpinnings. José Miguez-Bonino is a Christian who ac-

cepts the Marxist view of social and economic reality while insisting on a Christian framework. He calls the two strategic allies.
He believes that the criticism of religion is not essential to Marxism. He sees such criticism as not "primarily a general denuncia-
tion of religion as such—this is indeed a secondary, unoriginal
and quite questionable generalization—but as a very specific ex-
posure of the ideological function of the Christian religion and
particularly of protestantism, in relation to the individualistic,
egoistic and profit-crazed bourgeois world" (1976, p. 59). It could
be, Miguez-Bonino is saying, that the Marxist analysis of the
function of Christianity was close to the mark in nineteenth-
century Britain. Where Marxists err is in raising this analysis to a
philosophical principle. But it is difficult to see how Marxist
materialist and (therefore) atheistic assumptions can be so easily
dismissed as secondary, as Miguez seems to do. In fact, just after
the description of religion we quoted a moment ago, Marx himself claims that the criticism of religion is the premise for all other
criticism of society: "The criticism of religion is therefore the
germ of the criticism of the vale of tears whose halo is religion."
If man is to be free in the Marxist sense, religion must be done
away with.

It could be, of course, that some Marxist insights are valid—in
spite of their basic assumptions. Miguez-Bonino believes that this
is true and that the most important Marxist categories find validity only within a Christian framework. Specifically, the Marxist
view of the person is superficial and lacks the depth provided by
the Christian view. We will say more about this in our criticism
of Marxist philosophy below.

For the present it seems necessary to place the Marxist critique
of religion (and therefore of Christianity) as central in their analysis of society. Not only has religion no positive role to play in
history, it is destined to disappear when the conditions which
encourage it pass away. Again we quote Marx:

The religious reflection of the real world can, in any case, only
finally vanish when the practical relations of everyday life offer
to man none but perfectly intelligible and reasonable relations

to his fellowmen and to Nature. The life-process of society, i.e. the process of material production, will not shed its mystical veil until it becomes the product of freely associated men, and is consciously regulated by them in accordance with a settled plan. This, however, requires a definite material basis or set of conditions of existence which are themselves the spontaneous product of a long and painful process of development. (Marx, 1963, p. 120)

"Intelligible and reasonable relations," "freely associated men" are certainly glittering ideals; one wonders if Communism does not hold out a more substantive hope for people than any economic organization is able to provide. Can Marxists themselves avoid the charge of offering an ideology promising more than it can possibly provide?

The Christian Critique of Marxism

Contemporary Communism. Before criticizing the Communist system, let us make some general observations about contemporary Communist movements. Some would go so far as to say that Marxism as a creative movement is dead. The famous Polish philosopher Leszek Kolakowski, exiled from his post as professor of philosophy in Warsaw, wrote a few years ago: "In the Communist countries of Europe, Communist ideology is dead, in the sense that neither the rulers nor the ruled still take it seriously. For the ruling party, however, it is absolutely indispensable, since . . . it provides the only basis for legitimizing the tyranny of the single party system. . . . Nowadays, Communism is a matter of power and not of intellectual discussion" (Lutheran World Federation Newsletter, No. 19, July 1977). It is certainly impossible for anyone who has read Solzhenitsyn's account of Stalinist Russia, *The Gulag Archipelago,* to retain much confidence in the Communist movement in its Russian form.

For many others, however, Marxism still provides an intellectual stimulus that takes a variety of shapes according to the historical or cultural setting. Indeed one of the strengths of Marxism is its ability to adapt itself to widely differing circumstances. In fact so many expressions of Marxism and Leninism exist today that it is impossible to speak of a single Marxist ideology. Communists in North Korea, Vietnam, China and Cuba can all feel that their system is uniquely suited to their own needs. In many other countries, especially in Europe, various aspects of Marxist analysis continue to make an impact on the intelligentsia.

In short one should be careful not to overemphasize the success of Communism as a world movement today. Though in principle Communists may continue to mouth their goal of world domination—we will consider later how realistic a goal this is— in practice they have adapted themselves to the world economic system and more and more seek to get along with democratic nations. Peter Berger and others in fact have argued that the complex world economic system has rationalized and integrated relationships to such an extent that behavior between nations is rigidly prescribed and ideological concerns must play a very minor role. Capitalist and socialist countries must work with the system as it exists or they are not able to survive.

This suggests that on one level the confrontation is not really between Christianity and Marxism, but between capitalism and socialism (of which Marxism is a radical version). Christianity for its part does not provide an alternative political structure but rather offers values and a perspective by which to judge and evaluate any political system. Christians do not claim that any system represents the perfect form of government, though we are required to work to Christianize the order in which we find ourselves. Not all Christians agree in their evaluation of political systems. But surely all Christians would agree that both capitalism and Marxism, when they have failed, have failed in the same way: both have sometimes suggested that salvation is a matter of earthly and technical prosperity; both tend to absolutize the technological perspective and make an idol of a political system. Both must be shown that all human systems stand in the sphere of Christ's lordship and under the judgment of God's Word. We may have to support one or another system, but we do so with no illusion of having the mind of God. On balance, a study of the various kinds of socialist governments in the world today (there are over forty of them) would probably show that socialism has fared no better and no worse than capitalism in helping countries develop. At the same time, Christians in the West tend to over-look the fact that capitalism in the Third World is often more exploitative than it is in the West, not having undergone the reforms of the last hundred years of Western history.

By these considerations we do not mean to imply that Communism poses no threat to Christians today. This was brought home recently when a group of Christian students in Asia complained to their campus Christian workers that Communist fellow students were challenging them to present an alternative to the Marxist solution. Whatever our views of the matter, Marxism does have an explanation for the complex economic situation we face today, and for many people it makes sense. It speaks to people's concrete needs, to the day-to-day strivings of the disadvantaged. Are Christians unconcerned about these problems?

Christians then have two obligations in the face of the Communist challenge. We must first show, on Marxist assumptions, that the extravagant claims of Marxism are impossible. Second, we must show that Christianity provides a framework and a way of life in which all the proper concerns of Communists find their place. We will continue to speak of Marxism in general terms, as we have in introducing Marxist thought. We do this recognizing the many varieties and mutations of Marxism today, but also as a tribute to the psychological and intellectual appeal that classical Marxism continues to have for many thinking people, especially in the Third World.

The status of Marxist theory. First we turn to the Marxist system itself, examining problems associated with the status of Marxist theories and then asking some critical questions of the system. It is generally recognized that the most serious objection against Communism concerns the status of Marxist theory. Occasionally Communist theoreticians speak as if the historical process of economic forces were a historical fact; that is, as if an objective examination of historical facts would show that historical evolution took place according to Communist theory. Lenin claimed that Marx's view of history was a scientifically proven proposition, though strangely he admitted at least the possibility that the theory could be discredited. This ambivalence betrays the influence of Hegel's philosophy on Marx's thought (an influence prominent in all nineteenth-century historiography). Marx wished to employ a purely descriptive method in history, but, following Hegel, he could not give up the idea that history was moving toward a goal and that its development was fixed by its internal dynamics. Such a belief is surely something more than a scientific fact. But what could this more be?

Sometimes Communists appear to be speaking about the neutral development of technological methods, while at other times they seem to be speaking of a theory of society as a whole. This complex issue boils down to our earlier question: Can the Marxist method of economic analysis be separated from the larger philosophical framework in which it has usually appeared? If so, Christians could use it as an analytic tool within a Christian framework. But there is one telling objection against such a separation of Marxist theory. If all we have left is an objective analysis of what is taking place, how can we *urge* people to join the movement? If it is actually coming, it does not matter what you or I do; it will still happen. Marxists claim they are working with the forces of history. But how can Marx and Engels declare at the end of the *Communist Manifesto*, "Communists openly declare that their ends can be attained only by the forcible overthrow of all existing social conditions"? It seems that history needs our help to reach its certain goal. And despite our economic "conditionedness," we are free to choose the Communist option. Indeed Marxists here pay a backhanded compliment to religion by preaching their secular dream with evangelical fervor.

All this suggests that Communist theory is best understood as a philosophical commitment. Although it uses sociological analysis and scientific language, in the end it is not a statement of historical or sociological fact but a commitment to final meaning in the order of things. And in demanding this final commitment, it directly challenges Christianity. But if economic conditions are determinative, how can this commitment claim final status? With this question in mind we will seek to examine critically Marxist claims.

Critical questions about Marxism. Marxists insist that economic conditions determine human and social reality. It is easy to see why this point of view has made such a profound impact on modern history. Until Marx's time the economic factor was not recognized as important in human history. It was naively supposed that economic forces made no difference in people's lives and thus could be left to take care of themselves. This was clearly a mistake, and Marx was right to point it out. He saw clearly that the economic organization is vital to human life and social organization. But he went too far in asserting that it is the determinative element in society. Although economic structures are the sine qua non of society—no society can exist without them—it does not follow that they are a sufficient explanation for society as it exists. Marxists themselves include the ennoblement of man and freedom from suffering and oppression among their avowed goals. But according to Marxist theory, do not human degradation, suffering and oppression reflect necessary economic conditions? Why then should Marxists wish to interfere with the inevitable progress of history? The problem is poignantly illustrated by the confession of French Communist leader Roger Garaudy. Garaudy finds Christianity's answers outdated but admits that there is substance to the questions it seeks to respond to. When he is invited to speak on the problem of death, as a Marxist, Garaudy admits, " I arrive with empty hands" (Aptheker, p. 121).

Another question that can be directed against Communism is this: What would it take to disprove their thesis? No aspect of history can count against their point of view, because all fall short of the ideal, the classless society. Even in Communist countries the dictatorship of the proletariat has not yet given way to the classless society, so any imperfection that exists is explained as transitory. Meanwhile all the Marxists' humanist rhetoric is betrayed by the thousands of lives sacrificed in pursuit of their ends. There is no individual salvation, only the salvation of the community; therefore no individual concern can count against the validity of a determined history. At the same time Marxists also claim that all the faults of alternative systems are intrinsic and necessary to this stage of development. Conveniently they make all data support their own reading of history. A revisionist view of history (i.e., the Communist habit of rewriting history to suit their views) follows naturally from a revisionist view of the present. Many even in the Marxist camp are becoming cynical about such pretensions.

Finally we may ask about the plausibility of the classless society as the solution to all problems. According to Marx, the dialectic of history is moving toward a final settlement, a single synthesis in which all contradictions will be resolved. There is a nest of problems here: let us pick two for comment. First, in the light of contingency and human freedom, is it possible to read history so neatly? Of course Communists deny that there is such a thing as freedom. And yet, as we observed, they do not hesitate to seek people's "free" participation in their revolutionary activities. But can we really rejoice over the progress of history? Ironically this evolutionary view of history, once so popular, is now thoroughly discredited among practicing historians; there is too much that cannot be made to fit into such a schema. But the second problem is even more interesting. Why will the classless society be the final stage? Why will a process whose inner dynamic produces its own opposition suddenly stop functioning? Could it be that something of the Christian view of the final state has been smuggled into Marxism? We will follow this hint up momentarily; suffice it for now to point out that by a happy coincidence the Marxist heaven has become predictable on scientific and historical grounds. Perhaps a Marxist criticism of Christianity applies here: Communism seems to hold out hope for some pie in the sky by and by! Communists respond to this criticism by admitting that perhaps contradictions will exist, but they will be "non-antagonistic" since there will be no class distinctions.

But once again the Communist has made all the data point in his direction. We are told simply to believe that the perfect society can be evolved on this earth. And we wonder what existing society, what prophetic philosopher, what historical evidence could ever possibly lay sufficient ground for such a staggering claim.

The Christian alternative to the Marxist hope. Marxism has been called a Christian heresy. That is, all that Marx sought and wished for is possible only on the transcendent basis that the Christian faith provides. But Marx insisted on taking certain elements out of the Christian context and making his own grounds for them. Consider the following.

Marx's view of historical development clearly derives from the Christian view of providence. Christian's believe that a transcendent God personally directs the historical process. But God's direction is not such that secondary causes (such as human freedom) are overcome; rather they are made possible because of the moral structure built into creation and established in history. Thus history becomes not merely a deterministic process but a development of values which Christ calls "the kingdom of God, and his righteousness" (Mt 6:33 KJV). In this way religious values become not merely social constructions but the driving force of society.

This leads to the Marxist emphasis on man as maker of his destiny. The Marxist distinction between those who study history to know it and those who seek to change it is clearly based on Judeo-Christian values. It was the Greeks who studied as a way of knowledge; Christians insist that God's will is to be done and that—as Christ says—if we do this good thing, we will understand (Jn 17:7). Obedience is not an added extra to understanding; it is its heart and soul. Moreover in contrast to the Marxist goal of eliminating private property, Christians insist that the concrete world, though belonging to God, can be held in trust for future generations. As DeKoster points out, "The divorce between the individual and productive property is not healed by the classless society; it is rendered final and absolute!" (p. 47). For what is possessed by all is possessed by none. The Christian insists that property—whoever the manager or owner—exists foɪ the common good and thus should be a vehicle of community love and personal development.

Is it possible to realize ultimate human values in a Marxist context? It seems not. Marx believed human essence lay in the ability to make tools, and human agony, in alienation from material forces. Is the human problem alienation from the material environment or, as Christians insist, from God (and therefore from each other and the created world)? Christianity insists that the individual has supreme value and must always be seen as an end and not a means to some higher end. Such supreme value makes sense only in the context provided by the Christian view of a transcendent God and his creation. Still as relevant as the day it was uttered is Christ's assurance:

Are not five sparrows sold for two pennies?

And not one of them is forgotten before God.

Why, even the hairs of your head are all numbered.

Fear not; you are of more value than many sparrows.

(Lk 12:6-7)

Clearly Marxist weaknesses give no excuse for ignoring the problems of oppression and poverty that Marxists point to as evidence of capitalist failure. With their focus on the person, Christians should be the first to express concern for the destitute and the captive. Marxist analysis often correctly points out conditions that perpetuate poverty. Yet while we must struggle to solve such problems, we must not seek the solution by human efforts alone, but by engaging ourselves in God's mighty program of renewal and righteousness inaugurated in the mission of Christ.

We have hinted already that the Marxist vision of the classless society sounds suspiciously like the Christian idea of heaven. But unlike the Christian vision which provides present glimpses— what the Bible calls first fruits—of the future reality, the Marxist utopia is a deus ex machina, unlike anything we have previously known, which will one day stop the imperfect historical process The Christian wonders whether the vision of fulfillment in the classless society doesn't promise something more than the realization of human dreams. Does it not imply the end of history? Does it not, in other words, point to what can be realized only by God himself? It was Christianity that introduced such a hope into human thinking, but it was always a hope tied irrevocably to the person of our coming King, a hope gathering up within it all the Marxist wishes for and much more:

Therefore are they before the throne of God,
    and serve him day and night within his temple;
and he who sits upon the throne will shelter them
    with his presence.
They shall hunger no more;
neither thirst any more;
The sun shall not strike them, nor any scorching heat.
For the Lamb in the midst of the throne will be their shepherd,
and he will guide them to springs of living water;
and God will wipe away every tear from their eyes. (Rev 7:15-17)

Questions for Review

1. Describe the basic philosophical position of Karl Marx.
2. What does Marx mean by "alienation"? By "ideology"?
3. How did Marx alter Feuerbach's criticism of religion?
4. Discuss whether Marx's criticism of religion is essential to his view of society.
5. Discuss the relationship between Christian faith and both socialism and capitalism.
6. Give evidence that Communist theory is more a philosophical commitment than a scientific hypothesis.
7. Where was the Marxist evaluation of economic forces correct and where was it exaggerated?
8. Why is the Marxist idea of a classless society problematic?
9. How is the Marxist view of development derived from the Christian view of providence?
10. Compare and contrast the view of the person in Marxism and in Christianity.

CHAPTER ELEVEN

Epilog: Building Our Apologetic on Rock or on Sand

*W*e have completed our brief survey of Christian apologetics. We have seen that though serious objections have been raised against Christianity, none that we have surveyed constitutes a final barrier to faith. On the contrary we have seen that Christianity not only has an answer for its critics, but also provides a satisfying total perspective on the world as we experience it. In the end we must admit that all our evidence can also be read in other ways. We do not claim to have proved the truth of Christianity. Indeed no ultimate religious or philosophical commitment is subject to proof in the strict sense of the term. But neither can a religious commitment be postponed until all the evidence is in. William James laid this idol to rest when he said:

When I look at the religious question as it really puts itself to concrete men, and when I think of all the possibilities which both practically and theoretically it involves, then this command that we shall put a stopper on our heart, instincts, and courage, and wait—acting of course meanwhile more or less as if religion were not true—till doomsday, or till such time as our intellect and senses working together may have raked in evidence enough—this command, I say, seems to me the queerest idol ever manufactured in the philosophic cave. (pp. 60-61)

All we can fairly ask is that the kind and degree of evidence fit the case in question. We have argued that Christianity is best conceived of as the historical project in which God establishes his kingdom. This program will climax with the return of Christ and the renewal of creation. Accordingly we have proposed that historical evidence be adduced testifying to such a reality. Then we have argued that rational considerations may be employed to examine the Christian world view. When compared with alternative views, Christianity, we have claimed, provides a more satisfying framework for life and reality. But in the end, we have pointed out, final confirmation will not come until a person places his or her active faith in Christ as Lord and Savior. For in the end, this alone constitutes a proper response to reality. Only by faith can a person know the truth and do it.

We have sought to provide evidence in support of our claims, and Christians everywhere testify that in the process of commitment to Christ, the evidence mounts. In the view of this author, there is ample evidence to establish the truth of Christianity beyond reasonable doubt. Assurance, however, can come only as a special work of the Holy Spirit in the heart and life of the believer. Note that assurance is not a result of our reasoning; though reason must play a part, assurance is a gift of God. As Paul explains in Romans 8:16, "It is the Spirit himself bearing witness with our spirit that we are children of God."

Ultimately this confirming work of God must be understood as the foundation of our apologetic endeavors. If Christianity is God's project, then his glory and not the church's reputation is at stake. Christians have no need therefore to feel defensive.

Apologetics is not apologizing. The fact that many people do not believe in Christianity or are antagonistic to its claims may make us uncomfortable, but in itself it is no evidence against Christianity. The Scriptures never promise easy acceptance of the claims of the gospel. We have spoken of historical and cultural reasons for this unbelief. To all who dismiss the claims of Christ as incredible or impossible we offer this reminder from one of Montaigne's essays:

It is dangerous and presumptuous, besides the absurd temerity it implies, to disdain what we do not comprehend. For after you have established, according to your fine understanding, the limits of truth and falsehood, and it turns out that you must necessarily believe things even stranger than those you deny, you are obliged from then on to abandon them. (p. 33)

As G. K. Chesterton once said, if you cease to believe in God, you will not believe in nothing—you will believe anything.

All this defensiveness and uncertainty reflect a great reversal in modern times. We have come to respect argument and scientific evidence to such an extent that we look there first for religious assurance and comfort. So Christians nervously marshal their evidence, trying to subdue nagging doubts that their efforts may not be sufficient. We frantically scour history, science and archaeology for signs that Christianity might be true. Then when we have carefully constructed our arguments, when our barns are full of them, like the man in Christ's parable we say: "Soul, take your ease—Christianity is true." Are we not like the foolish man who built his house on sand?

Hebrew prophets in the Old Testament and the apostles in the New Testament would have been quite baffled by our approach. Their faith, as seen for example in Psalm 104, followed quite a different tack. There the rocks, springs and trees are not asked to support faith in God, but God is shown to make this created order possible.

No, we do not rest at night because of our wise apologetic but because our heavenly father cares for us and directs the course of creation and history. Because of him we can go to sleep knowing that we will wake to a world where science is possible, where art is a source of delight, where history is a tapestry meaningfully weaving together all the diverse strands of human life. Science, art and history are like so many streams flowing from a single source, streams from which we can drink freely with gratitude to the One who makes it all possible. We do not need more arguments, but eyes to see and ears to hear all the testimony around us to the glory of God. When this testimony is put in perspective, we will be like the wise man who built his house on the rock. When the rain and storms come, our house will stand firm because it is built on the rock. And into this great and strong house with its many rooms we invite our unbelieving and doubting friends.

Bibliography of Works Cited

Anderson, J. N. D.
    1969   *Christianity: The Witness of History.* London: Tyn-
                    dale Press.
    1970   *Christianity and Comparative Religion.* Downers
                    Grove, Ill.: InterVarsity Press.

Anselm of Canterbury
    1974-76   *Anselm of Canterbury,* 3 vols. Edited and translated
                    by Hopkins, Jasper, and Richardson. Toronto:
                    Edwin Mellen.

Aptheker, Herbert
    1970   *The Urgency of Marxist-Christian Dialogue.* New
                    York: Harper and Row.

Aquinas, Thomas
    1945   *Basic Writings.* Edited by Anton C. Pegis. New
                    York: Random House.

Armstrong, A. H., and
Markus, R. A.
    1960   *Christian Faith and Greek Philosophy.* New York:
                    Sheed and Ward.

Augustine of Hippo
    1958   *City of God.* Edited by V. J. Bourke. New York:
                    Doubleday.
    1960   *Confessions.* Translated by E. B. Pusey. New York:
                    Washington Square Press.

Ayer, A. J.
    1946   *Language, Truth and Logic.* 2d ed. New York:
                    Dover.

Baird, Robert D., and
Bloom, Alfred
1971   *Indian and Far Eastern Religious Traditions.* New
                             York: Harper and Row.

Barbour, Ian G.
1966   *Issues in Science and Religion.* New York: Harper
                             and Row.

Barth, Karl
1961   *The Humanity of God.* London: Collins.

Berdyaev, N.
1955   *The Meaning of the Creative Act.* New York: Harper
                             and Row.

Berger, Peter
1963   *Invitation to Sociology: A Humanistic Perspective.*
                             Garden City, N.Y.: Doubleday.
1969a   *The Sacred Canopy: Elements of a Sociological Theory
                             of Religion.* Garden City, N.Y.: Doubleday.
1969b   *A Rumor of Angels: Modern Society and the Redis-
                             covery of the Supernatural.* Garden City, N.Y.:
                             Doubleday.

Berger, Peter; Berger,
Brigitte; and Kellner,
Hansfried
1974   *The Homeless Mind: Modernization and Conscious-
                             ness.* Middlesex: Pelican Books.

Berkouwer, G. C.
1977   *A Half-Century of Theology.* Grand Rapids, Mich.:
                             Eerdmans.

Bhagavad Gita
1962   Translated by Juan Mascaró. Middlesex: Pen-
                             guin Books.

Bockmuehl, Klaus
1980   *The Challenge of Marxism: A Christian Response.*
                             Downers Grove, Ill.: InterVarsity Press.

Bouillard, Henri
1967   *The Logic of the Faith*. New York: Sheed and Ward.

Bouquet, A. C.
1967   *Comparative Religion*. 7th ed. Middlesex: Penguin Books.

Brown, Colin
1968   *Philosophy and the Christian Faith*. Downers Grove, Ill.: InterVarsity Press.

Bruce, F. F.
1959·   *The Apostolic Defense of the Gospel*. London: Inter-Varsity Press.

Burtt, E. A.
[1932] *The Metaphysical Foundations of Modern Science*. Rev. ed. Garden City, N.Y.: Doubleday.

Butler, Joseph
1736   *The Analogy of Religion, Natural and Revealed*. London: Printed for John and Paul Knopton.

Cairns, Earle
1973   *The Christian in Society*. Chicago: Moody Press.

Calvin, John
1949   *Commentary on the Psalms*. Translated by James Anderson. Grand Rapids, Mich.: Eerdmans.
1960   *The Institutes of the Christian Religion*. Edited by John McNeill. Philadelphia: Westminster.

Carnell, Edward John
1948   *An Introduction to Christian Apologetics*. Grand Rapids, Mich.: Eerdmans.
1957   *Christian Commitment*. New York: Macmillan.
1969   *The Case for Biblical Christianity*. Edited by Ronald Nash. Grand Rapids, Mich.: Eerdmans.

Chapman, Colin
1975   *Christianity on Trial*. Wheaton, Ill.: Tyndale House.

Clark, Gordon H.
1961   *Religion, Reason and Revelation*. Philadelphia: Pres-
               byterian and Reformed.
1964   *The Philosophy of Science and Belief in God*. Nutley,
               N.J.: Craig Press.

Coulson, C. A.
1958   *Science and Christian Belief*. London: Collins.

DeKoster, Lester
1956   *Communism and the Christian Faith*. Grand Rapids,
               Mich.: Eerdmans.

Dewey, John
1922   *Human Nature and Conduct*. New York: H. Holt.

Downs, F. S.
1976   *Christianity in North-East India*. Madras: Christian
               Literature Society.

Durkheim, Emile
1965 [1915]   *The Elementary Forms of the Religious Life*. New
               York: Macmillan Free Press.

Eddy, Mary Baker
1914   *Science and Health with Key to the Scriptures*. Boston:
               Allison V. Stewart.

Einstein, Albert
1956   *Out of My Later Years*. Secaucus, N.J.: Citadel.

Evans, C. Stephen
1977   *Preserving the Person: A Look at the Human Sciences*.
               Downers Grove, Ill.: InterVarsity Press.

Farrer, Austin
1972   *Reflective Faith*. Grand Rapids, Mich.: Eerdmans.

Feibleman, James K.
1976   *Understanding Oriental Philosophy*. New York:
               Mentor.

Feuerbach, Ludwig
1960 [1841]   *The Essence of Christianity.* New York: Harper and
                 Row.

Frend, W. H. C.
1965   *Martyrdom and Persecution in the Early Church.*
                 Oxford, England: Blackwell.

Freud, Sigmund
1964 [1927]   *The Future of an Illusion.* Edited by James Strachey.
                 Garden City, N.Y.: Doubleday.

Geehan, E. R., ed.
1971   *Jerusalem and Athens: Critical Discussion of the Phi-
                 losophy and Apologetics of Cornelius van Til.* Philadel-
                 phia: Presbyterian and Reformed.

Gelpi, D. J.
1976   *Charism and Sacrament.* New York: Paulist.

Gilkey, Langdon
1959   *Maker of Heaven and Earth: The Christian Doctrine
                 of Creation in the Light of Modern Knowledge.*
                 Garden City, N.Y.: Doubleday.

Gill, Jerry
1971   *The Possibility of Religious Knowledge.* Grand
                 Rapids, Mich.: Eerdmans.

Green, Michael
1968   *Runaway World.* London: Inter-Varsity Press.

Hackett, Stuart C.
1979   *Oriental Philosophy: A Westerner's Guide to Eastern
                 Thought.* Madison: University of Wisconsin Press.

Hesse, Mary
1954   *Science and the Human Imagination.* London: SCM.

Hick, John
1957   *Faith and Knowledge.* London: Collins.
1966   *Evil and the God of Love.* London: Collins.

1973a God and the Universe of Faith. New York: St. Martins.
1973b Philosophy of Religion. 2d ed. Englewood Cliffs, N.J.: Prentice-Hall.

Hoekema, Anthony A.
1979 The Bible and the Future. Grand Rapids, Mich.: Eerdmans.

Holmes, Arthur F.
1969 Christian Philosophy in the 20th Century: An Essay in Philosophical Methodology. Nutley, N.J.: Craig Press.
1971 Faith Seeks Understanding. Grand Rapids, Mich.: Eerdmans.
1977 All Truth Is God's Truth. Grand Rapids, Mich.: Eerdmans.

Hooykaas, R.
1972 Religion and the Rise of Modern Science. Grand Rapids, Mich.: Eerdmans.

Hume, David
1943 Dialogues Concerning Natural Religion. New York: Hafner.

Huxley, Julian
1957 [1929] Religion without Revelation. New York: Mentor.

James, William
1947 Essays on Faith and Morals. London: Longman, Green and Co.

Jeeves, M. A.
1967 Scientific Psychology and Christian Belief. London: Inter-Varsity Press.

Julian of Norwich
1977 Revelations of Divine Love. Garden City, N.Y.: Doubleday.

Justin Martyr
1953 Early Christian Fathers. Edited by Cyril C. Richardson. London: SCM.

Kant, Immanuel
1960   *Religion within the Limits of Reason Alone.* Trans-
                       lated and edited by T. M. Greene. New York:
                       Harper and Row.

Kierkegaard, Sören
1941   *Concluding Unscientific Postscript.* Princeton, N.J.:
                       Princeton University Press.
1954   *Fear and Trembling* and *Sickness unto Death.* Garden
                       City, N.Y.: Doubleday.

Koyama, Kosuke
1974   *Waterbuffalo Theology.* Maryknoll, N.Y.: Orbis
                       Books.
1976   *No Handle on the Cross.* London: SCM.

Kraemer, Hendrik
1958   *Theology of the Laity.* Philadelphia: Westminster

Krikorian, Yervant H., ed.
1944   *Naturalism and the Human Spirit.* New York:
                       Columbia University Press.

Krailscheimer, Alban.
1980   *Pascal.* New York: Hill and Wang, 1980.

Kuhn, Thomas
1970   *The Structure of Scientific Revolution.* 2d ed. Chi-
                       cago: University of Chicago Press.

Kuyper, Abraham
1968 [1898]   *Principles of Sacred Theology.* Grand Rapids, Mich.:
                       Eerdmans.

Latourette, Kenneth Scott
1962   *The 20th Century Outside Europe.* Vol. 5 of *Christian-
                       ity in a Revolutionary Age.* Grand Rapids, Mich.:
                       Zondervan.

Lessing, G.
1957   *Theological Writings.* Edited by H. Chadwick.
                       Stanford, Calif.: Stanford University Press.

Lewis, C. S.
1955   *Mere Christianity*. London: Collins.
1957   *The Problem of Pain*. London: Collins.
1960   *Miracles*. London: Collins.

Lindars, Bernadas
1961   *New Testament Apologetic: The Doctrinal Significance of Old Testament Quotations*. London: SCM.

Locke, John
1960   *An Essay Concerning Human Understanding*. London: Collins.

Lovelace, Richard F.
1979   *The Dynamics of Spiritual Life*. Downers Grove, Ill.: InterVarsity Press.

Luther, Martin
1902   *Table Talk*. Edited by William Hazlitt. London: Bell.
1953   *Commentary on Galatians*. London: James Clarke.
1967   *Selected Works*. Edited by T. G. Tappert. 4 vols. Philadelphia: Fortress Press.

Lyon, David
1979   *Karl Marx: A Christian Assessment of His Life and Thought*. Downers Grove, Ill.: InterVarsity Press.

MacKay, D. M.
1957   "Complementary Descriptions." *Mind* 66:390-94.

MacKay, D. M., ed.
1965   *Christianity in a Mechanistic World*. London: InterVarsity Press.

Marx, Karl
1932   *Capital and Other Writings*. New York: Random House.
1963   *Selected Writings in Sociology and Social Philosophy*. Edited by T. B. Bottomore and Maximilien Rubel. Middlesex: Penguin.

Marx, Karl, and Engels, F.
1948 [1848]   *The Communist Manifesto*. New York: International
                   Publishers.

Mascall, E. L.
1965   *Christian Theology and Natural Science*. Hamden,
                   Conn.: Archon.
1966   *He Who Is: A Study in Traditional Theism*. London:
                   Darton, Longman and Todd.

Matthews, Basil
1951   *Forward through the Ages*. New York: Friendship
                   Press.

Mercado, L.
1974   *Elements of Filipino Philosophy*. Tacloban, Leyte:
                   Divine Word University.

Miguez-Bonino, José
1975   *Doing Theology in a Revolutionary Situation*. Phila-
                   delphia: Fortress Press.
1976   *Christians and Marxists: The Mutual Challenge to
                   Revolution*. Grand Rapids, Mich.: Eerdmans.

Mitchell, Basil
1973   *The Justification of Religious Belief*. New York:
                   Seabury.

Moltmann, Jürgen
1981   *The Trinity and the Kingdom*. Edited and translated
                   by Margaret Kohl. San Francisco: Harper and
                   Row.

Montaigne, M. de
1948   *Selections from the Essays of Montaigne*. Edited and
                   translated by D. M. Frame. New York: Appleton-
                   Century-Crofts.

Montgomery, J. W.
1962   *The Shape of the Past: An Introduction to Philosophical
                   Historiography*. Ann Arbor, Mich.: Edwards.

1969   *Where Is History Going?* Grand Rapids, Mich.:
             Zondervan.

Morison, Frank
1958   *Who Moved the Stone?* Downers Grove, Ill.: Inter-
             Varsity Press.
Neill, S. C.
1961   *The Christian Faith and Other Faiths.* Oxford:
             Oxford University Press.

Newbigin, Lesslie
1978   *The Open Secret.* Grand Rapids, Mich.: Eerdmans.

Origen
1953   *Contra Celsus.* Translated by Henry Chadwick.
             Cambridge: Cambridge University Press.

Pascal, Blaise
1941   *Pensées.* New York: Modern Library.

Plantinga, Alvin
1974   *God, Freedom and Evil.* Grand Rapids, Mich.:
             Eerdmans.

Plato
1956   *The Works of Plato.* Edited by I. Edman. New York:
             Modern Library.

Polanyi, Michael
1964   *Personal Knowledge.* New York: Harper and Row.

Ramm, Bernard
1954   *The Christian View of Science and Scripture.* Grand
             Rapids, Mich.: Eerdmans.
1957   *Protestant Christian Evidences.* Chicago: Moody
             Press.
1965   *Varieties of Christian Apologetics.* 2d ed. Grand
             Rapids, Mich.: Baker.

Reid, J. K. S.
1969   *Christian Apologetics.* Grand Rapids, Mich.: Eerd-
             mans.

Richardson, Don
1974   *Peace Child.* Glendale, Calif.: Gospel Light.

Robinson, H. W.
1962   *The Christian Experience of the Holy Spirit.* London: Collins.

Ross, Nancy W.
1966   *Three Ways of Asian Wisdom.* New York: Simon and Schuster.

Russell, Bertrand
1967   *Why I Am Not a Christian.* New York: Simon and Schuster.
1969   *The ABC's of Relativity.* New York: New American Library.

Schaeffer, Francis A.
1968   *The God Who Is There.* Downers Grove, Ill.. Inter-Varsity Press.

Sire, James W.
1976   *The Universe Next Door: A Basic World View Catalog.* Downers Grove, Ill.: InterVarsity Press.

Skinner, B. F.
1971   *Beyond Freedom and Dignity.* New York: Vintage.

Smith, Huston
1958   *The Religions of Man.* New York: Harper and Row.

Song, Choan-Seng
1977   *Christian Mission in Reconstruction: An Asian Analysis.* Maryknoll, N.Y.: Orbis Books.

Stott, John R. W.
1975   *Christian Mission in the Modern World.* Downers Grove, Ill.: InterVarsity Press.

Strong, A. H.
1909   *Systematic Theology.* Philadelphia: Judson Press.

Tennant, F. R.

1928   *Philosophical Theology.* 2 vols. Cambridge: Cambridge University Press.

1943   *The Nature of Belief.* London: The Centenary Press.

Tertullian, Quintus

1931   *Apology.* Translated by T. R. Glover. New York: Putnam.

Thomas Aquinas   See Aquinas, Thomas.

Tillich, Paul

1963   *Systematic Theology.* Vol. 3. Chicago: University of Chicago Press.

Tippett, Alan R.

1967   *Solomon Islands Christianity: A Study in Growth and Obstruction.* New York: Friendship Press.

1969   *Verdict Theology in Missionary Theory.* Lincoln, Ill.: Lincoln Christian College Press.

Torrance, T. F.

1980   *The Ground and Grammar of Theology.* Belfast: Christian Journals.

Upanishads, The

1963   Translated by Swami Nikhilananda. New York: Harper and Row.

Van Til, Cornelius

1951   *Apologetics.* Philadelphia: Westminster Theological Seminary.

1952   *Christian Theistic Evidences.* Philadelphia: Westminster Theological Seminary.

1963   *Defense of the Faith.* 2d ed. Philadelphia: Presbyterian and Reformed.

Warfield, B. B.

1973   *Selected Shorter Writings.* Vol. 2, edited by J. E. Meeter. Philadelphia: Presbyterian and Reformed.

Watson, John F.
1930
Behaviorism. 3d ed. Chicago: University of Chicago Press.

Weber, Max
1946
From Max Weber: Essays in Sociology. Edited by H. H. Gerth and C. Wright Mills. New York: Oxford University Press.

Wendel, F.
1965
Calvin: The Origins and Development of His Religious Thought. London: Collins.

Whitehead, A. N.
1925
Science and the Modern World. New York: Macmillan.